In Touch

A BEGINNING COMMUNICATIVE COURSE

STUDENT BOOK 1

UPDATED AND IN COLOR

Oscar Castro • Victoria Kimbrough

Project Coordinator: Lyn McLean • Developmental Editor: Larry Anger
Consultants: Russell N. Campbell and William E. Rutherford

 Longman

 imnrc

In Touch Student Book 1

Longman, 95 Church Street, White Plains, N.Y. 10601

Instituto Mexicano Norteamericano de Relaciones Culturales, A.C., Hamburgo 115, Mexico 6, D.F.

Associated companies:
Longman Group Ltd., London
Longman Cheshire Pty., Melbourne
Longman Paul Pty., Auckland
Copp Clark Pitman, Toronto

We wish to thank the following for providing us with photographs:
Page 26, top left to right, bottom left and middle: Ross O'Loughlin; bottom right: Angel L. Cuevas. **Page 48:** Ross O'Loughlin. **Page 50:** New York University. **Page 62:** Ross O'Loughlin. **Page 83,** top left to right: Museum of Modern Art Film Still Archive; Lucasfilm Ltd./Museum of Modern Art Film Still Archive; Dell Publishing Co., Inc.; Random House Inc.; bottom left to right: Paramount Pictures Corporation/ Museum of Modern Art Film Still Archive; Museum of Modern Art Film Still Archive; Dell Publishing Co., Inc. **Page 84,** top: M. Giraudon; second row, left to right: ABKCO Records, Inc.; Polydor Inc.; Dan Serrano; third row, left to right: Universal Pictures/Museum of Modern Art Film Still Archive; Columbia Pictures Inc./ Museum of Modern Art Film Still Archive; United Artists Corporation/Museum of Modern Art Film Still Archive; bottom left to right: the John F. Kennedy Library, Waltham, Mass.; the Cosmos; Columbia Pictures Inc./Museum of Modern Art Film Still Archive.

We also wish to thank the following illustrators:
Pages 11 and 51: Anna Veltfort. **Pages 16, 69 and 75:** Tom Bloom. **Page 20,** middle: Tom Huffman. **Pages 30 and 34:** Rafael Barajas Durán. **Page 47,** bottom left, **Page 49,** bottom right, **Pages 52, 55 and 98:** Vladimir Yevtikhiev. **Page 56:** Enno Poersch.

Distributed in the United Kingdom by Longman Group Ltd., Longman House, Burnt Mill, Harlow, Essex CM2O 2JE, England and by associated companies, branches, and representatives throughout the world.

Project Editor: Marcie Miller
Character Illustrations: M.J. Quay
Cover Design Adaptation: Joseph DePinho
Cover Photography: Gayle Covner, Ross O'Loughlin, Oscar Castro, Victoria Kimbrough
Design: LMD Service for Publishers

ISBN: 0-8013-0918-2

1 2 3 4 5 6 7 8 9 10-WR-9695949392

Acknowledgments

We wish to acknowledge the valuable cooperation of the teaching and administrative staff of the Instituto Mexicano Norteamericano de Relaciones Culturales in Mexico City during the writing of this course.

We also wish to acknowledge the teachers who field-tested these materials in Mexico: Luis Abreu, Susana Bryan de Martinez, Clare M. Cedillo, Sergio Gaitan, Nina Guizar, Marianne Jung, John Lance, Isabella Marchese, Arturo Martin del Campo, Treasa Phillips, Margaret Snydelaar and Carolyn Vielma; in Brazil: Ana Maria Pedrosa de sa Freire de Souza; and in the United States: Marjorie Grayson, Dan Houston, Karen Riccardi and Judy Rothman.

We were very fortunate to have the help of Rafael Barajas Durán, who illustrated the pilot edition, and Ninfa Gonzalez and Lilia Gutierrez, who helped prepare the manuscript.

Jean Bodman and Milton G. Saltzer of the American Language Institute at New York University were extremely helpful in granting permission to use the Institute as a setting for the book.

We would especially like to thank Jane Sturtevant, Francisco Lozano, Alan McLean and Marcie Miller for their invaluable suggestions and contributions; Brian Abbs and Ingrid Freebairn for permitting us to adapt their Language Summary in *Starting Strategies* (Longman Group Ltd., London, 1978) for our own use; and Adrian Palmer and Margot Kimball for allowing us to adapt their Dialog Game in *Getting Along in English* (Longman Inc., New York, 1981).

We are also very grateful to all our friends and colleagues who encouraged and supported us.

Oscar Castro
Victoria Kimbrough

New York and Mexico

CONTENTS: SCOPE

UNIT	STRUCTURES	FUNCTIONS
1 pp. 1 to 6	**Present tense of** *be* *Am* (*'m*), *is* (*'s*), and *are* (*'re*) Information questions Affirmative statements	**Greeting people** Hello./Hi./Good morning./Good afternoon./Good evening. **Introducing yourself** My name's Maria./I'm Maria. **Introducing other people** Tony, this is Ali. **Meeting people** Nice to meet you./Glad to meet you. **Apologizing and accepting an apology** Excuse me. That's OK. **Asking for information** Where are you from? **Giving information about yourself** I'm from Mexico.
2 pp. 7 to 12	**Present tense of** *be* Information questions	**Asking for information** What's your name/address/telephone number? **Giving information about yourself** My name's Tony Costa. My address is 688 Columbus Avenue, Apartment 3F. My phone number is 373–6105. **Expressing agreement** That's right.
3 pp. 13 to 18	**Present tense of** *be* Yes/no questions Short answers **Subject pronouns** *I, you, he,* and *she* **Possessive adjectives** *My, your, his,* and *her* **Indefinite article** *A* and *an*	**Asking for information** What's his/her name? What do you do? Are you a secretary? **Giving information about yourself** I'm a secretary. **Giving information about other people** She's a secretary Her name's Sue Cleveland. **Expressing surprise** Really?

AND SEQUENCE

UNIT	STRUCTURES	FUNCTIONS

4
pp. 19 to 24

Demonstrative pronouns
This and *that*

Present tense of *be*
Word order: statements,
    questions, and short answers

Getting someone's attention and making a request
Excuse me! That's my pen.

Talking about possession
Is this your book?
Yes, it is./No, it isn't.

Apologizing
I'm sorry.

Expressing uncertainty
I think he's from Brazil.

5
pp. 25 to 32

Question formation
Yes/no questions and answers
Information questions and
    answers

**Regular and irrregular plurals of
nouns**

Possessive adjectives
My, *your*, *his*, *her*, *our*, *their*,
and *Tony's*

Asking for information about families
Are you married?
What does your father/mother do?

Giving information about families
My father's retired.
My sisters are secretaries.

Asking how to spell something
How do you spell it?

6
pp. 33 to 39

Indefinite pronoun
One

Present tense
Yes/no questions and answers

Subject pronouns
I, you, he, she, we, you, and
they

Identifying people
Who's that?/Who are they?
That's my father.

Asking for information about families
Do you have any brothers and sisters/children?
How old are your brothers and sisters/children?

Giving information about families
I have two brothers. One's twelve and one's fourteen.

**Review Unit
One**
pp. 40 to 46

Review of Units 1 through 6

Review of Units 1 through 6

UNIT	STRUCTURES	FUNCTIONS

7

pp. 47 to 53

There is and *there are*

Prepositions of location
On the corner of, *on*, *near*, and *between*

Asking for locations
Is there a bank near here?

Giving locations
There's one on Fifth Avenue.
There are two. One's on Broadway and one's on the corner of Fifth Avenue and Eighth Street.
Here's Fifth Avenue.

8

pp. 54 to 60

Prepositions of location
At, *on*, *next to*, *across from*, and *near*

Definite article *the*

Count and mass nouns
A vs. *some*

Offering to help someone
Can I help you?

Asking for locations
Where's the bookstore?
Where's that?
Where can I buy a map?

Giving locations
On 8th Street.
At the University Bookstore.

Thanking people
Thank you.

Accepting thanks
You're welcome.

9

pp. 61 to 67

Information questions and answers with *What time . . . ?* and *Where . . .?*

Have to and *has to*

Asking the time
What time is it, (please)?

Telling someone the time
It's 8:30.

Making a suggestion
Let's get something to eat.

Accepting a suggestion
OK, let's go.
That's a good idea.

Rejecting a suggestion
I'm sorry, I can't. I have to meet someone.

UNIT	STRUCTURES	FUNCTIONS

10
pp. 68 to 73

Would like

Count and mass nouns
 A vs. *some*
 A piece of, a cup of, and *a
  glass of*

Taking an order
 Are you ready to order?
 What would you like?
 Is that all?

Ordering something to eat
 I'd like a hamburger with lettuce and tomato.
 What kind of pie do you have?
 Apple pie, please.
 Could I have some french fries?

Asking about price
 How much is a piece of pie?

11
pp. 74 to 81

Prepositions of location
 On, at, and *in*

Present tense
 Questions and answers

Asking where someone lives
 Where do you live?

Saying where you live
 I live on West End Avenue.
 I live at 270 West End Avenue.
 I live in New York.

Asking personal questions
 Who do you live with?
 Don't you ever get lonely?
 What do you do in your free time?

12
pp. 82 to 89

Like and *like to*

Go + *-ing* (go swimming)

Frequency words
 Once a day (week, month)
 Every day (week, month)

Present tense
 Affirmative statements

Talking about likes and dislikes
 Do you like American TV?
 What kind of movies do you like?
 Who's your favorite actor?

Talking about frequency
 How often do you play tennis?
 (I play tennis) about once a week.

Inviting someone to do something
 Would you like to play tennis sometime?

Accepting an invitation
 Yes, I'd love to.

Refusing an invitation
 I'm sorry, I can't.

**Review Unit
Two**
pp. 90 to 99

Review of Units 6 through 12

Review of Units 6 through 12

Grammar Index   p. 100

Word List   pp. 101 to 104

INTRODUCING . . .

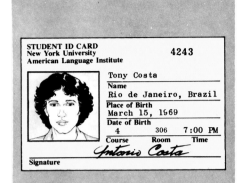

STUDENT ID CARD
New York University
American Language Institute

4243

Name: Tony Costa
Place of Birth: Rio de Janeiro, Brazil
Date of Birth: March 15, 1969

Course	Room	Time
4	306	7:00 PM

Signature: *Antonio Costa*

STUDENT ID CARD
New York University
American Language Institute

6703

Name: Maria Sanchez
Place of Birth: Mexico City, Mexico
Date of Birth: February 21, 1965

Course	Room	Time
4	306	7:00 PM

Signature: *Maria Sanchez*

STUDENT ID CARD
New York University
American Language Institute

7735

Name: Jeannette Kaba
Place of Birth: Abidjan, Ivory Coast
Date of Birth: June 28, 1962

Course	Room	Time
4	306	7:00 PM

Signature: *Jeannette Kaba*

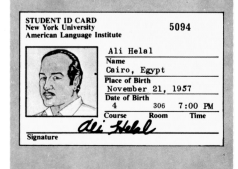

STUDENT ID CARD
New York University
American Language Institute

5094

Name: Ali Helal
Place of Birth: Cairo, Egypt
Date of Birth: November 21, 1957

Course	Room	Time
4	306	7:00 PM

Signature: *Ali Helal*

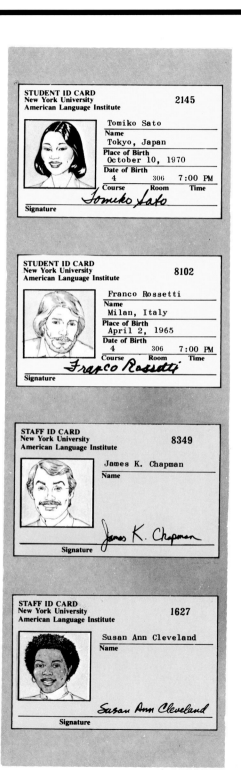

STUDENT ID CARD
New York University
American Language Institute

2145

Name: Tomiko Sato
Place of Birth: Tokyo, Japan
Date of Birth: October 10, 1970

Course	Room	Time
4	306	7:00 PM

Signature: *Tomiko Sato*

STUDENT ID CARD
New York University
American Language Institute

8102

Name: Franco Rossetti
Place of Birth: Milan, Italy
Date of Birth: April 2, 1965

Course	Room	Time
4	306	7:00 PM

Signature: *Franco Rossetti*

STAFF ID CARD
New York University
American Language Institute

8349

Name: James K. Chapman

Signature: *James K. Chapman*

STAFF ID CARD
New York University
American Language Institute

1627

Name: Susan Ann Cleveland

Signature: *Susan Ann Cleveland*

Nice to meet you.

Tony and Maria are at the American Language Institute.

Tony:	**Oh, excuse me.**
Maria:	**That's OK.**
Tony:	**What course are you in?**
Maria:	**English 4.**
Tony:	**Me too.**
Maria:	**We're all in English 4. This is Ali. . .**
Ali:	**Nice to meet you.**
Maria:	**Jeannette . . .**
Jeannette:	**Hi.**
Maria:	**and Tomiko.**
Tomiko:	**Hello.**
Maria:	**And my name's Maria.**
Tony:	**Hi. I'm Tony.**
Maria:	**Where are you from, Tony?**
Tony:	**Brazil. What about you?**
Maria:	**I'm from Mexico.**

Answer *That's right* **or** *That's wrong.*

1. Tony's from Brazil. *That's right.*
2. Maria's from Brazil too. *That's wrong.*
3. Tony's in English 3.
4. Jeannette and Tomiko are in English 4.

1

PRACTICE 1

Introduce yourself.

A: Hello. My name's ....
B: Hi. I'm ....

NOTE:
You can greet people like this:
Hi.
Hello.
Good morning.
Good afternoon.
Good evening.

PRACTICE 2

Introduce other people.

A: ...., this is ....
B: Nice to meet you.
C: Nice to meet you too.

You Can Also Say:
Glad to meet you.

PRACTICE 3

Ask someone where he's/she's from.
Tell someone where you're from.

Maria: Where are you from?
Tony: I'm from Brazil. What about you?
Maria: I'm from Mexico.

A: Where are you from?
B: .... What about you?
A: I'm from ....

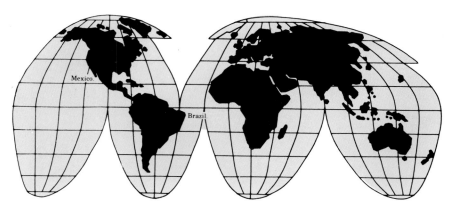

PRACTICE 4 Write *'m, 's* or *'re*.

Maria: Hello. My name .... Maria and
        this is Jeannette.
Tony: Nice to meet you. I .... Tony.
Maria: What course are you in, Tony?
Tony: English 4.
Maria: We .... in English 4 too.
        Where are you from?
Tony: Brazil. What about you?
Maria: I .... from Mexico. Jeannette ....
        from the Ivory Coast.

PRACTICE 5 Open Conversation: practice
this conversation with a partner.

A: My name's ....
B: I'm ....
A: Nice to meet you.
B: ....
A: Where are you from, ...?
B: .... What about you?
A: ....

EXPANSION

ZERO	ONE	TWO	THREE	FOUR	FIVE	SIX	SEVEN	EIGHT	NINE	TEN
0	1	2	3	4	5	6	7	8	9	10

 PRACTICE 6 Read the identification
number to your partner.
Your partner will tell you
the name of the person.

A: 5094
B: Ali Helal

NOTE:

5094 = five – oh – nine – four

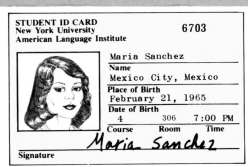

STUDENT ID CARD
New York University
American Language Institute   6703

Name: Maria Sanchez
Place of Birth: Mexico City, Mexico
Date of Birth: February 21, 1965
Course: 4   Room: 306   Time: 7:00 PM
Signature: *Maria Sanchez*

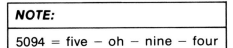

STAFF ID CARD
New York University
American Language Institute   8349

Name: James K. Chapman
Signature: *James K. Chapman*

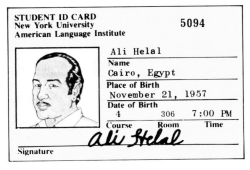

STUDENT ID CARD
New York University
American Language Institute   5094

Name: Ali Helal
Place of Birth: Cairo, Egypt
Date of Birth: November 21, 1957
Course: 4   Room: 306   Time: 7:00 PM
Signature: *Ali Helal*

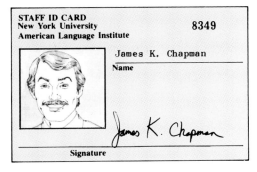

STAFF ID CARD
New York University
American Language Institute   1627

Name: Susan Ann Cleveland
Signature: *Susan Ann Cleveland*

STUDENT ID CARD
New York University
American Language Institute   2145

Name: Tomiko Sato
Place of Birth: Tokyo, Japan
Date of Birth: October 10, 1970
Course: 4   Room: 306   Time: 7:00 PM
Signature: *Tomiko Sato*

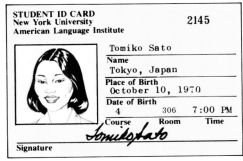

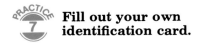 **Fill out your own identification card.**

The months of the year are:

January	July
February	August
March	September
April	October
May	November
June	December

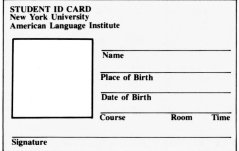

STUDENT ID CARD
New York University
American Language Institute

Name

Place of Birth

Date of Birth

Course   Room   Time

Signature

 Do the crossword puzzle.

ACROSS	DOWN
1. **3**	1. **2**
2. **4**	2. **5**
3. **7**	3. **6**
4. **10**	4. **8**
5. **0**	5. **9**
	6. **1**

 Jim Chapman is talking to another teacher at the American Language Institute. Listen and answer the questions.

Where is Karen Thomas from?

....

Where is Jim Chapman from?

....

HOW MUCH DO YOU KNOW?

1. Complete the Conversation

Ali: Good morning, Maria.
Maria: Hello, Ali.
Ali: ....?
Maria: I'm in English 4 now. Ali, this ....
        Tony Costa.
Ali: ....
Tony: Nice to meet you too.
Ali: ....?
Tony: I'm from Brazil.

2. Find the Conversations

Here are two conversations. Read the conversations with your partner. You read part **A** and cover part **B**. Your partner reads part **B** and covers part **A**. Listen to your partner before you answer.

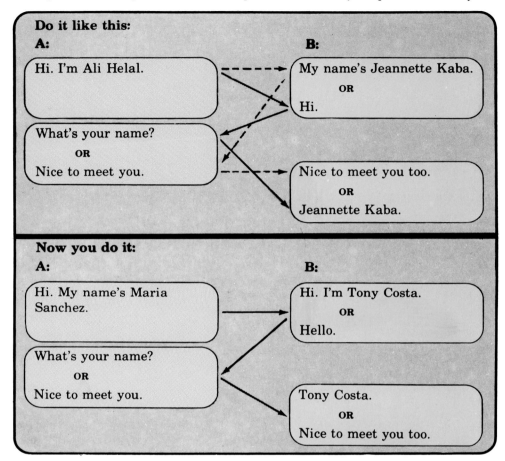

Do it like this:

A:

Hi. I'm Ali Helal.

What's your name?
OR
Nice to meet you.

B:

My name's Jeannette Kaba.
OR
Hi.

Nice to meet you too.
OR
Jeannette Kaba.

Now you do it:

A:

Hi. My name's Maria Sanchez.

What's your name?
OR
Nice to meet you.

B:

Hi. I'm Tony Costa.
OR
Hello.

Tony Costa.
OR
Nice to meet you too.

3. Circle the correct answer:

1. Nice to meet you.
   a) English 3.
   b) Nice to meet you too.
   c) What about you?

2. I'm from Brazil. What about you?
   a) I'm Maria.
   b) I'm in English 4.
   c) I'm from Mexico.

3. What course are you in?
   a) That's OK.
   b) Next, please.
   c) English 4.

4. Where are you from?
   a) English 4.
   b) Brazil.
   c) Tony.

5. This is Jeannette.
   a) Me too.
   b) That's OK.
   c) Nice to meet you.

6. I'm Maria.
   a) What about you?
   b) That's OK.
   c) Hi. My name's Tony.

LANGUAGE SUMMARY

Now You Can Do This:

greet people:	Hello./Hi./Good morning./Good afternoon./Good evening.
introduce yourself:	My name's Maria./I'm Maria.
introduce people:	Tony, this is Ali.
meet people:	Nice to meet you./Glad to meet you.
apologize:	Excuse me.
accept an apology:	That's OK.
ask for information:	Where are you from? What course are you in?
give information about yourself:	I'm from Mexico. I'm in English 4.

Grammar

Be: am ('m), is ('s), are ('re)

I	'm	
My name	's	Maria.
This	is	
We	're	in English 4.

Information Questions ⟶ And Answers

Where			from?
		are you	
What course			in?

I	'm	from Mexico.
		in English 4.

Useful Words and Expressions

'm, 's, is, are (v) *
meet (v)
•
name
•
you
I
this
•
my
your
•

nice
•
too
•
what
where
•
to
from
about
•

Hello.
Hi.
Nice to meet you.
That's right.
That's wrong.
Zero, one, two, three, four, five, six, seven, eight, nine, ten.

* (v) = *verb*

What's your name and address?

Tony's at registration.

Sue:	What's your name?
Tony:	Antonio Costa.
Sue:	Your address?
Tony:	688 Columbus Avenue, Apartment 3F.
Sue:	And your phone number?
Tony:	Excuse me?
Sue:	What's your telephone number?
Tony:	Oh, it's 373-6105.
Sue:	And where are you from?
Tony:	Brazil.
Sue:	And you're in English 4?
Tony:	Yes, that's right.
Sue:	Sign here, please. . . . Thank you.
Tony:	You're welcome.
Sue:	Next, please.
Tony:	Goodbye, Maria. See you later, Tomiko.
Maria:	Bye, Tony.
Tomiko:	Bye.

REGISTRATION FORM
AMERICAN LANGUAGE INSTITUTE · NEW YORK UNIVERSITY

(MR.) MISS
MRS. MS. **NAME:** Costa   Antonio
　　　　　　　　　　(Last)　　　　(First)　　　　(Middle)

ADDRESS: 688   Columbus Avenue
　　　　　　　(Street)

New York   N. Y.   10025
(City)   (State)   (Zip)

HOME TELEPHONE: 373-6105   **SEX:** (M) F

OCCUPATION: restaurant employee   **DATE OF BIRTH:** March 15, 1969
　　　　　　　　　　　　　　　　　　　　　　(Month)　(Day)　(Year)

PLACE OF BIRTH: Rio de Janeiro, Brazil   **COURSE:** English 4

SIGNATURE: *Antonio Costa*   **DATE:** Sept. 3, 1989

Answer *That's right* **or** *That's wrong.*

1. Tony's in English 1.
2. Tony's in Brazil.
3. Tony is Antonio Costa.

**Ask someone what his/her name is.
Tell someone your name.**

A: What's your name?
B: ....

**Ask someone what his/her telephone
number is. Tell someone your
telephone number.**

Sue: What's your telephone number?
Tony: It's 3-7-3 6-1-oh-5.

A: What's your telephone number?
B: (It's) .... *or* I don't
have a phone.

ELEVEN	TWELVE	THIRTEEN	FOURTEEN	FIFTEEN	SIXTEEN	SEVENTEEN	EIGHTEEN	NINETEEN
11	12	13	14	15	16	17	18	19

TWENTY	TWENTY-ONE	THIRTY	THIRTY-TWO	FORTY	FORTY-THREE	FIFTY	FIFTY-FOUR	SIXTY	SIXTY-FIVE
20	21	30	32	40	43	50	54	60	65

SEVENTY	SEVENTY-SIX	EIGHTY	EIGHTY-SEVEN	NINETY	NINETY-EIGHT	ONE HUNDRED	TWO HUNDRED AND NINE
70	76	80	87	90	98	100	209

**Read the addresses in Tony
Costa's address book.**

**Ask someone what his/her address
is. Tell someone your address.**

Sue: What's your address?
Tony: 688 Columbus Avenue.

A: What's your address?
B: (It's) ....

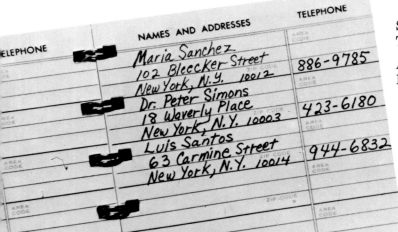

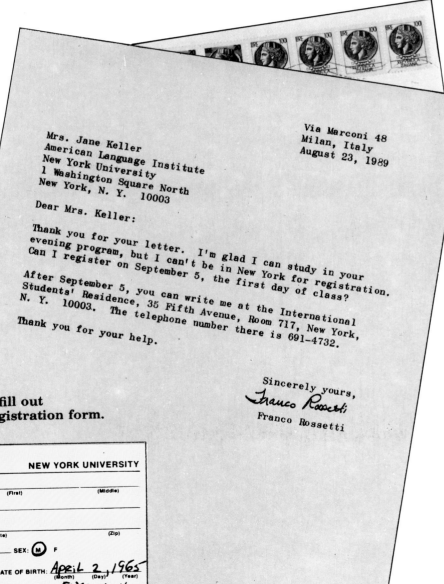

PRACTICE 5 Open Conversation: ask for information for your address book.

A: What's your name?
B: ....
A: What's your address?
B: ....
A: And your telephone number?
B: ....

NAME AND ADDRESS	TELEPHONE
	AREA CODE
	NUMBER
	AREA CODE
	NUMBER

EXPANSION

Via Marconi 48
Milan, Italy
August 23, 1989

Mrs. Jane Keller
American Language Institute
New York University
1 Washington Square North
New York, N. Y. 10003

Dear Mrs. Keller:

Thank you for your letter. I'm glad I can study in your evening program, but I can't be in New York for registration. Can I register on September 5, the first day of class?

After September 5, you can write me at the International Students' Residence, 35 Fifth Avenue, Room 717, New York, N. Y. 10003. The telephone number there is 691-4732.

Thank you for your help.

Sincerely yours,

Franco Rossetti

Franco Rossetti

PRACTICE 6 Read the letter and fill out Franco Rossetti's registration form.

REGISTRATION FORM
AMERICAN LANGUAGE INSTITUTE   **NEW YORK UNIVERSITY**

MR. MISS
MRS. MS.   NAME: _____
                        (Last)   (First)   (Middle)

ADDRESS: _____
                    (Street)

_____
     (City)   (State)   (Zip)

HOME TELEPHONE: _____ SEX: Ⓜ F

OCCUPATION: _Student and Hotel Clerk_   DATE OF BIRTH: _April 2, 1965_
                                                                        (Month) (Day) (Year)

PLACE OF BIRTH: _Milan, Italy_   COURSE: _English 4_

SIGNATURE: _____ DATE: _____

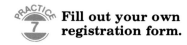 **Fill out your own registration form.**

NOTE:

Mr. Chapman
Mrs. Kaba or Ms. Kaba
Miss Thomas or Ms. Thomas

REGISTRATION FORM
AMERICAN LANGUAGE INSTITUTE   **NEW YORK UNIVERSITY**

MR.   MISS
MRS.   MS.   NAME: _____
                            (Last)   (First)   (Middle)

ADDRESS: _____
                    (Street)

_____
            (City)   (State)   (Zip)

HOME TELEPHONE: _____ SEX: M   F

OCCUPATION: _____ DATE OF BIRTH: _____
                                                                    (Month)   (Day)   (Year)

PLACE OF BIRTH: _____ COURSE: _____

SIGNATURE: _____ DATE: _____

This is the answer to Franco's letter. Write capital letters where necessary.

New York University

The American Language Institute
1 Washington Square North, Room 10
New York, N.Y. 10003
Telephone: (212) 598-3931

august 30, 1989

M. F   R
Mr. Franco Rossetti
35 fifth avenue, room 717
new york, new york 10003

dear mr. rossetti:

    i'm pleased to tell you that you can register
for the evening program on september 5. you can
take the placement examination on september 5 too.
the examination begins at six o'clock. please
fill out the enclosed registration form and bring
it with you.

                                            sincerely,
                                            Jane Keller
                                            (mrs.) jane keller

 Listen to the conversation and fill in Maria's address book.

Addresses

NAME _____

ADDRESS _____ Madison Avenue, Apt. _____

TEL. NO. _____

HOW MUCH DO YOU KNOW?

1. Complete the Conversation

Tony: ....
Maria: My name's Maria Sanchez.
Tony: ....?
Maria: Mexico. What about you?
Tony: ....?

Maria: English 4.
Tony: ....?
Maria: 886-9785.
Tony: ....?
Maria: 102 Bleecker Street.

2. Find the Conversations

Here are two conversations. Read the conversations with your partner. You read part **A** and cover part **B**. Your partner reads part **B** and covers part **A**. Listen to your partner before you answer.

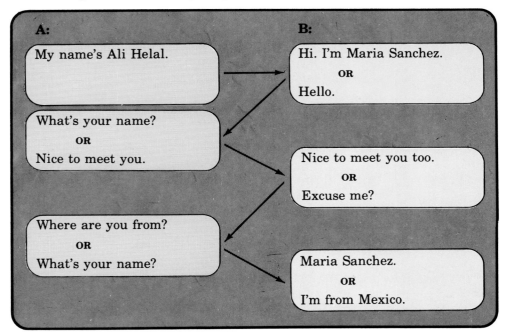

3. Circle the Answer

1. What's your address?
   a) Brazil.
   b) I don't have one.
   c) 688 Columbus Avenue.

2. What's your telephone number?
   a) Thank you.
   b) 886-9785.
   c) Maria Sanchez.

3. Where are you from?
   a) Italy.
   b) That's OK.
   c) Tomiko Sato.

4. Goodbye.
   a) Hello.
   b) That's OK.
   c) See you later.

5. Thank you.
   a) Brazil.
   b) You're welcome.
   c) I'm from Japan.

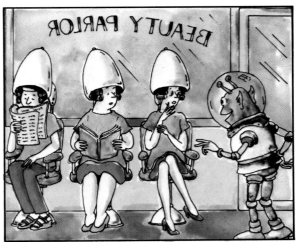

"And where are you from?"

11

LANGUAGE SUMMARY

Now You Can Do This:

ask for information: What's your name/address/telephone number?

give information
about yourself: My name's Tony Costa.
My address is 688 Columbus Avenue, Apartment 3F.
My phone number is 373-6105.

express agreement: That's right.

Grammar

Information Questions ————➤ And Answers

What's	your	last name?	Costa.
		address?	688 Columbus Avenue.
		phone number?	373-6105.

Useful Words and Expressions

don't
excuse (v)
have (v)
•
phone
telephone number
address
•

it
me
•
a
last
•
and
•

Excuse me?
Eleven, twelve, thirteen, fourteen,
fifteen, sixteen, seventeen, eighteen,
nineteen, twenty, twenty-one, thirty,
thirty- two, forty, forty-three, fifty,
fifty-four, sixty, sixty-five, seventy,
seventy-six, eighty, eighty-seven, ninety,
ninety-eight, one hundred,
two hundred and nine.

What do you do?

Tony and Tomiko are in a coffee shop.

Tony:	Say, what's her name?
Tomiko:	That's Sue Cleveland. She's a secretary at the American Language Institute.
Tony:	And who's that?
Tomiko:	I don't know. I think he's a teacher.

Waitress:	What would you like?
Tomiko:	Coffee, please.
Tony:	Coffee for me too. What do you do, Tomiko?
Tomiko:	I'm a secretary. What about you?
Tony:	I work in a restaurant.
Tomiko:	Oh, really?
Tony:	Yeah. I work for my uncle.

Answer *That's right* **or** *That's wrong.*

1. Tomiko and Sue are secretaries.
2. Tony and Sue are friends.

Ask someone what his/her occupation is. Tell someone your occupation.

Tony: What do you do?
Tomiko: I'm a secretary.

A: What do you do?
B: I'm a/an ....

Find someone with your occupation. Ask and answer like this:

Maria: Are you a teacher?
Sue: No, I'm a secretary.

A: Are you a ....?
B: No, I'm a/an ....
    or Yes, I am.

Write *a* or *an*.

Foreign Students Register at the American Language Institute

From right to left: Ali Helal, ... engineer from Egypt; Maria Sanchez, ...student in hotel administration from Mexico; Jeannette Kaba, ... nurse from the Ivory Coast; Tomiko Sato, ... secretary from Japan; and Oscar Delgado, ... accountant from Venezuela.

PRACTICE 4 Ask and say who other people are like this:

Tony: Say, what's her name?
Tomiko: That's Sue Cleveland. She's a secretary at the American Language Institute.

A: (Say), what's his/her name?
B: (That's) .... He's/She's a/an
.... *or* I don't know.

PRACTICE 6 Open Conversation

A: What's his/her name?
B: ....
A: Oh, that's right. He's/She's ....
B: No, he's/she's ....

PRACTICE 5 Write his/her.

Tony: What's .... name?
Tomiko: Jeannette Kaba.
Tony: Is she a teacher at the American Language Institute?
Tomiko: No, she's a student.
Tony: And is that .... boyfriend?
Tomiko: No, I think that's .... husband.
Tony: What's .... name?
Tomiko: Dossou, I think.
Tony: Is he a student here too?
Tomiko: I don't know.

EXPANSION

PRACTICE 7 Read the newspaper article about Jeannette Kaba. Then write an article about Ali Helal.

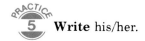

University News
SEPTEMBER 6, 1989

JEANNETTE KABA is a new foreign student at the American Language Institute. She's in English 4. Mrs. Kaba is from the Ivory Coast. She's a nurse and her husband is a medical student at Columbia Medical School. Their daughter Yemi is with them in New York.

REGISTRATION FORM
AMERICAN LANGUAGE INSTITUTE   **NEW YORK UNIVERSITY**

MR. MISS MRS. MS.   NAME: HELAL   ALI
                              (Last)   (First)   (Middle)

ADDRESS: 35   FIFTH AVENUE
                  (Street)
NEW YORK   NEW YORK   10003
(City)   (State)   (Zip)

HOME TELEPHONE: 691-4732   SEX: Ⓜ F

OCCUPATION: ENGINEER   DATE OF BIRTH: 11 21 57
                                              (Month) (Day) (Year)

PLACE OF BIRTH: CAIRO, EGYPT   COURSE: ENGLISH 4

SIGNATURE: Ali Helal   DATE: 9/3/89

Ali Helal .... new foreign student at .... He's in English .... Mr. .... is .... He's .... Mr. Helal's wife and son are both in Egypt. .... wife, Magda, works for Air Egypt, and .... son, Anwar, is in the third grade.

Now write an article about a friend.

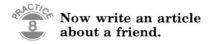

 Jim and Sue are talking about a new teacher. Listen and answer.

What do Sue and Karen do?

Sue's a ....

Karen's a ....

 Introduce people like this:

Tomiko: Tony, this is Sue Cleveland.
          She's a secretary at the American
          Language Institute.
Tony: Nice to meet you, Sue.
Sue: Hi.

A: ...., this is ....
    He's/She's a ....

B: Nice to meet you, ...
    or Hello, ...

C: Hi.

"And what do you do?"

HOW MUCH DO YOU KNOW?

1. Complete the Conversation

Ali: ....?
Jeannette: Jeannette Kaba.
Ali: .... teacher?
Jeannette: No, I'm a nurse. ....?
Ali: I'm an engineer. ....?
Jeannette: My husband and I are from the
             Ivory Coast.

2. Find the Conversations

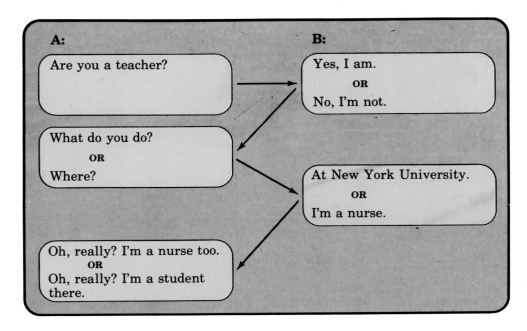

A:

Are you a teacher?

What do you do?
OR
Where?

Oh, really? I'm a nurse too.
OR
Oh, really? I'm a student there.

B:

Yes, I am.
OR
No, I'm not.

At New York University.
OR
I'm a nurse.

3. Circle the Answer

1. Are you a teacher?
   a) No, he's a taxi driver.
   b) No, she's a doctor.
   c) No, I'm an engineer.

2. She's a secretary.
   a) What's your name?
   b) What's her name?
   c) What's his name?

3. What do you do?
   a) Nice to meet you too.
   b) Brazil.
   c) I'm a secretary.

4. This is Jeannette.
   She's a nurse.
   a) Thank you, Jeannette.
   b) Nice to meet you, Jeannette.
   c) That's OK, Jeannette.

LANGUAGE SUMMARY

Now You Can Do This:

ask for information:	What's his/her name?
	What do you do?
	Are you a secretary?
give information about yourself:	I'm a secretary.
give information about people:	She's a secretary.
	Her name's Sue Cleveland.
say you don't know:	I don't know.
get someone's attention:	Say.
express surprise:	Really?

Grammar

Yes/No Questions ⟶ And Answers

Are you an engineer?

No, **I'm** a secretary.
Yes, I am./No, I'm not.

Pronouns

I'm (I am) a secretary.
He's (He is) an engineer.
She's (She is) a teacher.

Possessive Adjectives

My name's Sue.
His name's Ali.
Her name's Karen.
What's **your** name?

Indefinite Article: **a/an**

a secretary
an engineer

Useful Words and Expressions

am (**v**)	nurse	he	not
do (**v**)	secretary	she	there
know (**v**)	student	•	•
•	teacher	her	at
	doctor	his	•
	engineer	•	Yes.
	taxi driver	an	No.
	waitress	the	Oh, really?
	accountant	•	What do you do?
	•		

UNIT 4

Excuse me! That's my book.

Tony and Tomiko are in a coffee shop.
Jim and Sue are in the coffee shop too.

Tomiko:	**There's Maria and Ali. Let's go say hello.**
Tony:	**OK.**
Mr. Chapman:	**Excuse me! That's my book.**
Tony:	**No, it isn't. Look, here's my name.**
Sue:	**Jim, is this your book?**
Mr. Chapman:	**Oh, I guess it is. I'm really sorry.**
Tony:	**That's OK.**

Mr. Chapman:	**Who's that?**
Sue:	**That's Antonio Costa.**
Mr. Chapman:	**Is he a student at the ALI?**
Sue:	**Uh-huh.**
Mr. Chapman:	**Where's he from?**
Sue:	**I think he's from Brazil.**

Answer *That's right* **or** *That's wrong.*

1. Tony has Mr. Chapman's book.
2. Sue and Tony are friends.
3. Sue has Jim's book.
4. Tony's a student at the American Language Institute.

Someone has your *book/pen/*.............................
Ask for it like this:

A: Excuse me! That's my ....
B: Oh. I'm sorry.
A: That's OK.

NOTE: *this/that*

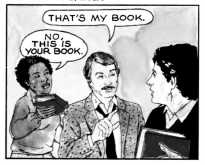

You Can Also Say:
A: Excuse me! That's my book.
B: No, it isn't. Look, here's my name.
A: Oh. I'm sorry.
B: That's OK.

 Find the owner. Ask and answer like this:

Sue: Is this your book?
Mr. Chapman: Oh. I guess it is.

A: Is this your ....?
B: Oh. I guess it is. *or*
    Yes, it is. *or* No, it isn't.

 Ask and say who other people are.

Mr. Chapman: Who's that?
Sue: That's Antonio Costa.

A: Who's that?
B: That's ....

sweater
coat
dictionary
notebook
purse
pencil
wallet
pen
umbrella
briefcase

 Ask for information about other people.

Mr. Chapman: Is he a student?
Sue: Uh-huh.

A: Is he/she a/an ....?
B: Uh-huh. *or*
    No, he's/she's a/an ....

 Ask and say where other people are from.

Mr. Chapman: Where's he from?
Sue: I think he's from Brazil.

A: Where's he/she from?
B: I think he's/she's from .... *or*
    He's/She's from .... *or* I don't know.

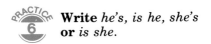 **Write** *he's, is he, she's* **or** *is she.*

Tomiko: Ali's from Egypt.
Tony: .... a student?
Tomiko: Yes, ... an English student at the American Language Institute.
Tony: .... in Mr. Chapman's class?
Tomiko: Uh–huh.
Tony: What about his friend Maria? .... in Mr. Chapman's class too?
Tomiko: Yes, I think .... in his class.

 **Open Conversation**

A: Who's that?
B: ....
A: Is he/she a/an ....?
B: ....
A: Where's he/she from?
B: ....

EXPANSION

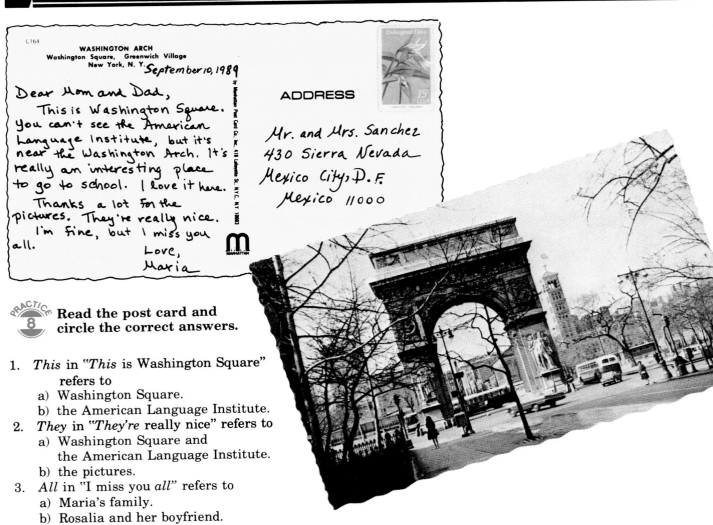

C164

WASHINGTON ARCH
Washington Square, Greenwich Village
New York, N.Y. *September 10, 1989*

Dear Mom and Dad,
This is Washington Square. You can't see the American Language Institute, but it's near the Washington Arch. It's really an interesting place to go to school. I love it here.
Thanks a lot for the pictures. They're really nice.
I'm fine, but I miss you all.
Love,
Maria

by Manhattan Post Card Co., Inc. 118 Lafayette St., N.Y.C., N.Y. 10003

ADDRESS

Mr. and Mrs. Sanchez
430 Sierra Nevada
Mexico City, D.F.
Mexico 11000

Read the post card and circle the correct answers.

1. *This* in *"This* is Washington Square" refers to
   a) Washington Square.
   b) the American Language Institute.
2. *They* in *"They're* really nice" refers to
   a) Washington Square and the American Language Institute.
   b) the pictures.
3. *All* in "I miss you *all*" refers to
   a) Maria's family.
   b) Rosalia and her boyfriend.

9 Fill in the blanks with a period (.) or a question mark (?).

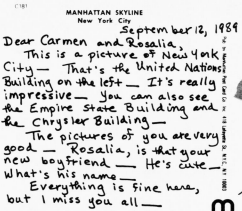

C181

MANHATTAN SKYLINE
New York City

September 12, 1989

Dear Carmen and Rosalia,

This is a picture of New York City ___ That's the United Nations Building on the left ___ It's really impressive ___ You can also see the Empire State Building and the Chrysler Building ___

The pictures of you are very good ___ Rosalia, is that your new boyfriend ___ He's cute ___ What's his name ___

Everything is fine here, but I miss you all ___

Love,
Maria

Carmen a...
Sanchez
430 Sierra Nevada ___
Mexico City, D.F.
Mexico 11000

10 Complete the post card.

___
(date)

Dear ___,
This is a picture of ___. That's ___.
It's ___. You can also see ___.
Everything ___ here, but ___ you.
Love,
___

15¢
OLIVER
WENDELL
HOLMES

___
(name)
___
(address)

11 Sue and Mr. Chapman are talking about a student. Listen and complete the sentences.

1. The student's from ....
2. His name's ....
3. Mr. Chapman's his ....

HOW MUCH DO YOU KNOW?

1. Complete the Conversation

Mr. Chapman:	....?
Sue:	Jeannette Kaba.
Mr. Chapman:	....?
Sue:	The Ivory Coast.
Mr. Chapman:	....?
Sue:	No, she's a nurse.
Mr. Chapman:	....?
Sue:	855-8899.
Mr. Chapman:	....?
Sue:	66 Madison Avenue.

2. Find the Conversations

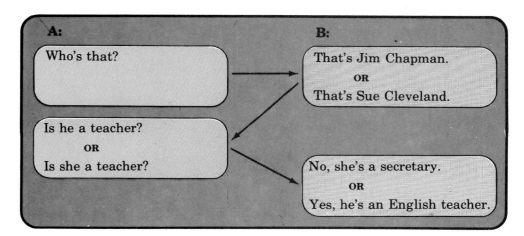

A:
Who's that?

Is he a teacher?
OR
Is she a teacher?

B:
That's Jim Chapman.
OR
That's Sue Cleveland.

No, she's a secretary.
OR
Yes, he's an English teacher.

3. Circle the Answer

1. I'm a secretary. What about you?
   a) I'm sorry.
   b) I'm from the Ivory Coast.
   c) I'm an accountant.

2. Excuse me! That's my book.
   a) That's OK.
   b) See you later.
   c) I'm sorry.

3. Who's that?
   a) I think it's my book.
   b) I think he's a teacher at the ALI.
   c) I'm a doctor.

4. What's his name?
   a) Sue.
   b) Tony.
   c) Mr. Chapman and Sue.

5. Is Tomiko a teacher?
   a) No, she's a teacher.
   b) No, she's a secretary.
   c) No, she's from Japan.

LANGUAGE SUMMARY
Now You Can Do This:

get someone's attention and make a request:	Excuse me! That's my pen.
ask for information and identify:	Is this your book? Yes, it is./No, it isn't.
apologize:	I'm sorry.
express uncertainty:	I think he's from Brazil.

Grammar

Demonstrative Pronouns

Who's **that?**	**That's** Antonio Costa.
Is **this** your book? Is **that** your pen?	Yes, it is./No, it isn't.

Word Order: Statements and Questions ⟶ And Short Answers

	He/She	**'s**	a student.
Is	he/she		a student?
	This	**is**	your book.
Is	this		your book?

Yeah.
Yes, it is./No, it isn't.

Pronouns

I'm	(**I** am)	
You're	(**You** are)	a student.
He's	(**He** is)	from the Ivory Coast.
She's	(**She** is)	

Useful Words and Expressions

isn't (v)	book	*pen*	sorry
think (v)	*coat*	*purse*	English
•	*briefcase*	*wallet*	•
	umbrella	*pencil*	who
	sweater	•	•
	dictionary	*that*	I'm sorry.
	notebook		OK.

Here are some pictures of my family.

Ali asks Maria about pictures of her family.

Ali:	Do you have any pictures of your family?
Maria:	Yes, I have some here somewhere. Yeah, here they are. This is my father with my twin sisters, Carmen and Rosalia. They're both bilingual secretaries.
Ali:	What does your father do?
Maria:	He's retired. This is my mother. She's a lawyer.
Ali:	Really?
Maria:	Uh-huh. And these are my brothers, Pepe and Ricardo, and that's Carmen's boyfriend, Raul Sanchez.
Ali:	His last name's Sanchez too?
Maria:	Yes. It's a very common name in Mexico. What's your last name?
Ali:	Helal.
Maria:	How do you spell it?
Ali:	H-E-L-A-L.
Maria:	Is that a common name in Egypt?
Ali:	Yes. It means "moon" in Arabic. My wife's maiden name is Helal too.
Maria:	Oh, are you married?
Ali:	Yes. And I have a seven-year-old son. What about you?
Maria:	No, I'm not married.
Ali:	Do you have a boyfriend?
Maria:	No, I don't.

Answer *That's right* or *That's wrong.*

1. Maria's father is a lawyer.
2. Maria's boyfriend is in Mexico.
3. Maria's sisters speak two languages.

Ask someone how to spell his/her last name. Spell your last name.

Maria: What's your last name?
Ali: Helal.
Maria: How do you spell it?
Ali: H-E-L-A-L.

A: What's your last name?
B: ....
A: How do you spell it?
B: ....

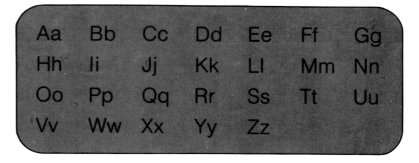

 Talk about marital status.

Maria: Are you married?
Ali: Yes, I am.

A: Are you married?
B: Yes, I am. *or* No, I'm not.

If someone isn't married, you can continue like this:

A: Do you have a boyfriend/girlfriend?
B: Yes, I do. *or* No, I don't.

You Can Also Say:
No, I'm single.
No, I'm divorced.
I'm separated.
My husband died two years ago.

 Talk about other people's occupations.

Ali: What does your mother do?
Maria: She's a lawyer.

A: What does your .... do?
B: He's/She's a/an ....

NOTE:
He's **a** teacher.

He's **a** secretary.

She's **a** waitress.

They're teacher**s**.

They're secreta**ries**.

They're waitress**es**.

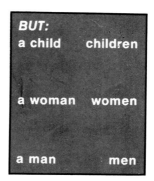
BUT:
a child   children

a woman   women

a man   men

**Maria is asking Ali about his family. Write
a or *an* only where necessary.**

Maria: What about your family, Ali?
Ali: Well, my wife's .... accountant for Air Egypt,
        and our son's .... student in the
        third grade. They're in Cairo with my parents.
Maria: Do you have any brothers or sisters?
Ali: Yes, two brothers and one sister.
Maria: What do they do?
Ali: My brother, Ibrahim, and my sister, Aziza,
        are .... students, and my brother, Sherif, works with
        my father. They're .... salesmen.
Maria: What does your mother do?
Ali: She's .... housewife.

 **Do you remember their occupations?
Ask and answer like this:**

A: What do they do?
B: They're ....
A: What does he/she do?
B: He's/She's a/an ....

Ali's brother Sherif
and his father

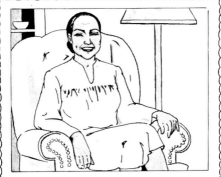

Ali's mother Noura

Maria's sisters Carmen
and Rosalia

Ali's wife Magda

Ali's brother Ibrahim and his sister Aziza

Maria's mother Ana

6 **Make a list of the occupations in your class. Ask and answer like this:**

A: What do you do?
B: I'm a secretary.
A: What does he/she do?
B: He's/She's a teacher.

7 **Open Conversation**

A: What's his/her last name?
B: ....
A: How do you spell it?
B: ....
A: What does .... do?
B: ....

LIST OF OCCUPATIONS			
NUMBER	OCCUPATION	NUMBER	OCCUPATION
1	Teacher		
	Secretaries		

Read the list of occupations.

EXPANSION

8 **Read the questions first, then read the newspaper article. Underline the answers to the questions like this:**

1. What does Mr. Chapman do?

~~20, 1979—Jan Chapman, son of Mr. and Mrs. Charles Chapm of Los Angeles, is now an English <u>teacher</u> at Ne York University in New York City. Mr. Chapma a graduate of Santa Monica High School s~~

2. What are Mr. Chapman's children's names?

3. Where is Mr. Chapman from?

EVENING REVIEW

James Chapman teaches in New York City

LOS ANGELES, August 20, 1989—James Chapman, son of Mr. and Mrs. Charles Chapman of Los Angeles, is now an English teacher at New York University in New York City. Mr. Chapman is a graduate of Santa Monica High School and UCLA. His job is a little different from most English teachers' jobs because he teaches English to foreign students, and he has students from ten different countries in his classes. Mr. Chapman's daughter, Maryann, and his son, Peter, are with him in New York City. Maryann is in the second grade and Peter is in the fourth grade.

Capitalize means "write capital letters." *Punctuate* means "write periods (.), question marks (?), and commas (,)." Capitalize and punctuate the following paragraph. Check your work with the newspaper article in Practice 8.

karen thomas daughter of mr and mrs norman thomas of los angeles is now an english teacher at new york university in new york city ms thomas is a graduate of hollywood high school and ucla her job is a little different from most english teachers' jobs because she teaches english to foreign students and she has students from ten different countries in her classes

Ask what things mean like this:

A: What does UCLA mean?

B: It means University of California at Los Angeles.

United States of America

United Nations

Television

Very Important Person

Trans World Airlines

American Language Institute

New York University

Unidentified Flying Object

11 Listen to the spelling of these words and write them.

1) .... 2) .... 3) ....
4) .... 5) .... 6) ....

Now write the words under *family* **or** *professions*.

FAMILY	PROFESSIONS

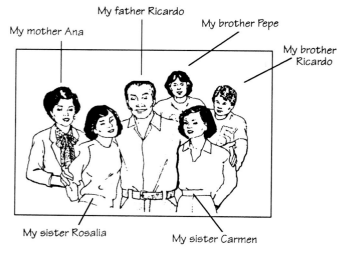

My mother Ana · My father Ricardo · My brother Pepe · My brother Ricardo · My sister Rosalia · My sister Carmen

"Do you have any pictures of your family?"

HOW MUCH DO YOU KNOW?

1. Complete the Conversation

Karen: Is that a new student?
Jim: Yes.
Karen: ....?
Jim: Jeannette.
Karen: ....?
Jim: Kaba.

Karen: ....?
Jim: K-A-B-A.
Karen: ....?
Jim: The Ivory Coast.
Karen: ....?
Jim: She's a nurse.

2. Find the Conversations

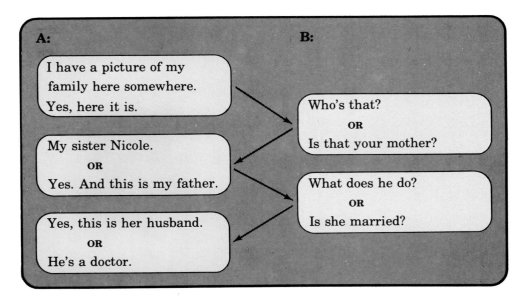

A: **B:**

I have a picture of my
family here somewhere.
Yes, here it is.

Who's that?
OR
Is that your mother?

My sister Nicole.
OR
Yes. And this is my father.

What does he do?
OR
Is she married?

Yes, this is her husband.
OR
He's a doctor.

3. Circle the Answer

1. What does your father do?
   a) Yes, he is.
   b) He's married.
   c) He's a lawyer.

2. What's your last name?
   a) Tony.
   b) Costa.
   c) Tony Costa.

3. Do you have a boyfriend?
   a) No, I have a boyfriend.
   b) No, I'm a student.
   c) No, I'm married.

4. How do you spell his name?
   a) His name's Dossou.
   b) D-O-S-S-O-U.
   c) N-A-M-E.

5. Are they engineers?
   a) No, they're salesmen.
   b) E-N-G-I-N-E-E-R-S.
   c) No, they're engineers.

LANGUAGE SUMMARY

Now You Can Do This:

ask for information about families: Are you married?
What does your father/mother do?

give information about families: My father's retired.
My sisters are secretaries.

ask how to spell something: How do you spell it?

Grammar

Yes/No Questions ⟶ And Answers

Are	you	
	they	married?
Is	he/she	

Yes, I	**am.**/No, I'm **not.**
Yes, they	**are.**/No, they **aren't.**
Yes, he/she	**is.**/No, he/she **isn't.**

Information Questions ⟶ And Answers

What	**do**	you	**do?**
What	**does**	your father	**do?**
How	**do**	you	**spell** Helal?

I'm	a	student.
He's		retired.
H-E-L-A-L.		

Regular Plural

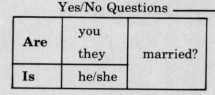

Most nouns:

Nouns ending in
-z, -s, -ch, -sh:

Nouns ending in **y:**

Ali's	an	engineer.
They're		engineers.
She's	a	waitress.
They're		waitresses.
Carmen's	a	secretary.
They're		secreta**ries.**

Irregular Plural

a woman	**women**
a man	**men**
a child	**children**

Possessive Adjectives

That's	**my** **your** **his** **her** **our** **their** **Tony's**	house.

Useful Words and Expressions

're (are) (v)	father	*children*	lawyer	•	Aa, Bb, Cc, Dd, Ee, Ff,
mean (v)	mother	*twin*	doctor	somewhere	Gg, Hh, Ii, Jj, Kk, Ll,
does	brother	*son*	picture	here	Mm, Nn, Oo, Pp, Qq, Rr,
spell (v)	sister	*daughter*	•	•	Ss, Tt, Uu, Vv, Ww, Xx,
•	husband	boyfriend	they	how	Yy, Zz.
	wife	girlfriend	•	•	
			married	of	

Do you have any brothers and sisters?

Maria goes to the ladies' room.
Tomiko and Tony say hello to Ali.

Maria:	Where's the ladies' room?
Ali:	Over there, next to the telephones.
Maria:	Excuse me for a minute. I'll be right back.
Tomiko:	Hi, Ali!
Ali:	Hi, Tomiko. Hi, Tony. How are you?
Tony:	Fine, thanks. And you?
Ali:	Oh, I'm fine. Sit down.
Tomiko:	Thanks. What are those?
Ali:	They're pictures of Maria's family.
Tomiko:	Can I see them?
Ali:	Sure. This is Maria's mother.
Tomiko:	And who are they?
Ali:	Her brothers.
Tomiko:	They're cute. How old are they?
Ali:	I think one's twelve and one's fourteen. Do you have any brothers and sisters?
Tomiko:	I have a sister.
Tony:	How old is she?
Tomiko:	Twenty-four.

Answer *That's right* or *That's wrong.*

1. The ladies' room is next to the telephones.
2. Tomiko has two brothers.
3. Tomiko's sister is twelve years old.

33

1 **Greet someone like this:**

Ali: Hi, Tony. How are you?
Tony: Fine, thanks. And you?
Ali: I'm fine.

A: Hi, ... How are you?
B: .... And you?
A: ....

You Can Also Say:
(I'm)   OK.   all right.   pretty good.   very well.

 2 **Talk about brothers and sisters/children like this:**

Ali: Do you have any brothers and sisters?
Tomiko: I have a sister.

A: Do you have any brothers and sisters/children?
B: I have .... *or* No, I don't.

 3 **Talk about the ages of brothers and sisters/children.**

Ali: How old is your sister?
Tomiko: She's twenty-four.

Ali: How old are your brothers?
Maria: One's twelve and one's fourteen.

A: How old is/are ....?
B: ....

 4 **Talk about the occupations of brothers and sisters/children.**

Maria: What does your sister do?
Ali: She's a student.

Maria: What do your brothers do?
Ali: One's a salesman and one's a student.

A: What does/do .... do?
B: ....

Talk about pictures of someone's family.

A: Who's that?/Who are they?

B: ....

Open Conversation

A: Do you have any ....?

B: I have ....

A: How old is/are ....?

B: ....

A: What does/do ....do?

B: ....

This is the first paragraph of a letter from Tomiko's mother. The letter is about Tomiko's sister, Akiko. Complete the letter with *is* or *are*.

September 28, 1989

Dear Tomiko,

This ___ a quick note to send you this article from the Asahi Times. Now you know why I can't write more often. I'm so busy. Akiko and her husband and children ___ fine. The children ___ both in school and, of course, Akiko ___ very happy about that; now she has some free time. Michiko ___ a lovely little girl but her brother, Taro ___ a little devil. Of course, he ___ only six.

EXPANSION

TUESDAY, SEPT. 12, 1989

Asahi Times

Hanako Sato, New Director of Elizabeth Eden

Tokyo — Hanako Sato, a well-known businesswoman, is the new director of *Elizabeth Eden*, an international cosmetics company with two offices in Japan. Mrs. Sato is the first woman to direct the com-

pany's Tokyo office in its fifteen-year history. Mrs. Sato is also a successful housewife and mother. She and her husband, Taro Sato, have two daughters. Tomiko, 19, is a secretary for Japan Air Lines in New York City. Akiko, 24, lives here in Tokyo with her husband and two children.

PRACTICE 8 Read the newspaper article about Mrs. Sato and underline the answers to these questions like this:

1. What does Mrs. Sato do?

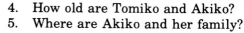

new director of *Elizabeth Eden*, an international cosmetics

2. What's *Elizabeth Eden*?
3. What's Mrs. Sato's husband's name?
4. How old are Tomiko and Akiko?
5. Where are Akiko and her family?

PRACTICE 9 This is the second paragraph of the letter from Tomiko's mother. There are five sentences in the paragraph. Punctuate and capitalize the sentences.

your father is fine he's at home right now and he says hello i'm fine too but i have a lot of work we all miss you write soon.   love
                    mother

Listen and circle the numbers you hear.

Elizabeth Eden is a large international cosmetics company. The Tokyo office has ⟨219⟩ 290 employees. Here are some of their jobs.

13   30   are executives.
15   50   are secretaries.
16   60   are accountants.
14   40   are salespeople.
15   50   are receptionists.
17   70   are in the advertising department.
18   80   are chemists.

HOW MUCH DO YOU KNOW?

1.   Complete the Conversation

Ali: ....?
Tony: My mother and father.
Ali: ....?
Tony: I have two brothers.
Ali: ....?
Tony: One's an accountant and one's a doctor.
Ali: ....?
Tony: One's twenty-two and one's twenty-
        seven.

2.   Find the Conversations

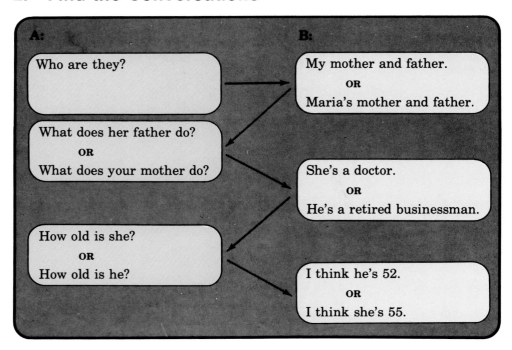

3. Look at the pictures and do the crossword puzzle.

ACROSS

1. He's Tomiko's ....

2. She's Tomiko's ....

3. She's Mr. and Mrs. Sato's ....

DOWN

1. She's Mr. Sato's ....

2. He's Mrs. Sato's ....

3. She's Tomiko's ....

4. Circle the Answer

1. Who are they?
   a) Maria's parents.
   b) Maria.
   c) Maria's a student.

2. What do your brothers do?
   a) They're salesmen.
   b) They're OK.
   c) They're married.

3. Is he married?
   a) No, he's from Brazil.
   b) Yes, he's single.
   c) Yes, his wife's in Egypt.

4. Do you have any sisters?
   a) Yes, I have two brothers.
   b) No, but I have two sisters.
   c) Yes, I have three.

5. How old is your brother?
   a) June 14, 1968.
   b) 19.
   c) Fine, thank you.

LANGUAGE SUMMARY

Now You Can Do This:

identify:	Who's that?/Who are they? That's my father.
ask for information about families:	Do you have any brothers and sisters/children?/ How old are your brothers and sisters/children?
give information about families:	I have two brothers. One's twelve and one's fourteen.

Grammar

Indefinite Pronoun: **One**

I have two brothers.

One's a student and **one**'s an accountant.

Yes/No Questions ⟶ And Answers

Do you **have** any brothers and sisters?

No, I **don't**./Yes, I **do**.

Yes, I **have** a brother and two sisters.

Pronouns

I	'm	a student.
He **She**	's	from the Ivory Coast.
We **You** **They**	're	students. from the Ivory Coast.

Useful Words and Expressions

businessman
children
salesman
- one
- 's (**possessive**)
fine

old
retired
any

How are you?
Fine, thanks. And you?
How old is/are ....?

Making friends

Ali and Tony are talking in Washington Square.

Ali: Where are you from?
Tony: Brazil.
Ali: And where's your family—here or in Brazil?
Tony: In Brazil.
Ali: What does your father do?
Tony: He's a businessman. He has a restaurant in Rio.
Ali: Do you have any brothers and sisters?
Tony: I have two brothers. One's an accountant and one's a doctor.
Ali: How old are they?
Tony: Twenty-two and twenty-seven.

Answer *That's right* **or** *That's wrong.*

1. Tony's parents are in Brazil.
2. His father is a doctor.
3. Mr. and Mrs. Costa have three daughters.
4. Tony's brothers are twenty-two and twenty-seven.

1 Talk about families. Ask and answer like this:

Ali: Where's your family?
Tony: In Brazil.
Ali: What does your father do?
Tony: He's a businessman.

A: Where's your family?
B: In ....
A: What does/do ....?
B: ....

2 Talk about brothers and sisters/children. Ask and answer like this:

Ali: Do you have any brothers and sisters?
Tony: I have two brothers. One's an accountant
       and one's a doctor.
Ali: How old are they?
Tony: Twenty-two and twenty-seven.

A: Do you have any brothers and sisters/children?
B: I have .... *or* No, I don't.
A: How old is/are ....?
B: ....

3 Complete the conversation and practice it with a partner.

Tony: My name's Tony Costa.
Ali: ....
       1. I'm from Egypt.
       2. I'm Ali Helal.
       3. I'm in English 4.

Tony: ....
       1. Where are you from?
       2. Egypt.
       3. Where's that?

Ali: ....
       1. Egypt.
       2. I'm in English 4.
       3. I don't know.

Tony: ....
       1. Why not?
       2. Are you in English 3?
       3. Who's that?

Ali: ....
       1. No, I'm married.
       2. No, I have two brothers.
       3. No, English 4.

PRACTICE 4 This is part of a letter from Tony's mother. Read the paragraph and answer the questions.

> Here's a picture of Mario's new girlfriend. Her name's Carmen Diaz and she's an architect here in Rio. She's from Argentina. Her family's really unusual. Everyone except Carmen works for an airline. Her father's a pilot, her mother's a reservations agent, and her sister and brother are flight attendants. They're all in Buenos Aires.

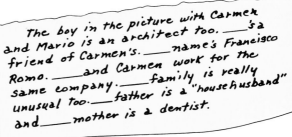

1. *Her* in "*her* family's really unusual" refers to:
   a) Carmen's mother.
   b) Carmen.
2. *They* in "*they*'re in Buenos Aires" refers to:
   a) Carmen's family.
   b) Carmen and Mario.
3. *Except Carmen* in "Everyone *except Carmen* works for an airline" means
   a) and Carmen.
   b) not Carmen.

PRACTICE 5 Here is another paragraph in the letter from Tony's mother. Complete the paragraph.

> The boy in the picture with Carmen and Mario is an architect too. ____'s a friend of Carmen's. ____ name's Francisco Romo. ____ and Carmen work for the same company. ____ family is really unusual too. ____ father is a "househusband" and ____ mother is a dentist.

Jim Chapman meets Maria Sanchez in the University Coffee Shop.

Mr. Chapman:	Excuse me, is this your notebook?
Maria:	Yes, I guess it is. Thanks.
Mr. Chapman:	You're welcome. Are you a student here?
Maria:	Uh-huh. What about you?
Mr. Chapman:	I'm a teacher. My name's Jim Chapman.
Maria:	Hi. I'm Maria Sanchez.
Mr. Chapman:	What course are you in, Maria?
Maria:	English 4.
Mr. Chapman:	Oh, I'm your teacher.
Maria:	Really?
Mr. Chapman:	Yeah. Would you like a cup of coffee?
Maria:	OK.

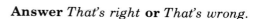

Answer *That's right* **or** *That's wrong*.

1. Jim has Maria's notebook.
2. *Uh-huh* means "yes."
3. Maria would like a cup of coffee.

Find the owner. Ask and answer like this:

Mr. Chapman: Excuse me, is this your notebook?
Maria: Yes, I guess it is.

A: Excuse me, is this your ....?
B: Yes, I guess it is. *or* No, it isn't.

 Complete the conversation and practice it with a partner.

Maria: This is a picture of my family.
Mr. Chapman: ....
1. What's that?
2. Who's that?
3. Where's that?

Maria: ....
1. My sister Carmen.
2. She's married.
3. She's a doctor.

Mr. Chapman: ....
1. What do you do?
2. What does she do?
3. What's her name?

Maria: ....
1. She's in Mexico.
2. She's from Mexico.
3. She's a secretary.

Mr. Chapman: ....
1. Is she married?
2. Is she a doctor?
3. Is she your sister?

Maria: ....
1. No, she's twenty-five years old.
2. No, she isn't.
3. No, she's in the picture.

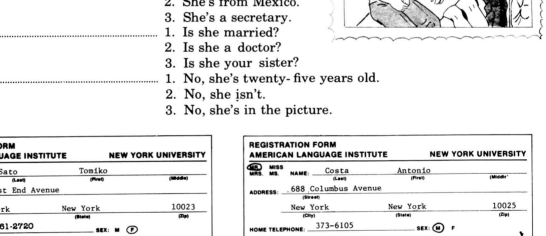 **Ask someone about his/her occupation. Tell someone your occupation.**

Mr. Chapman: Are you a student?
Maria: Yes. What about you?
Mr. Chapman: I'm a teacher.

A: Are you a ....?
B: Yes. *or*
   No, I'm a .... What about you?
A: I'm a ....

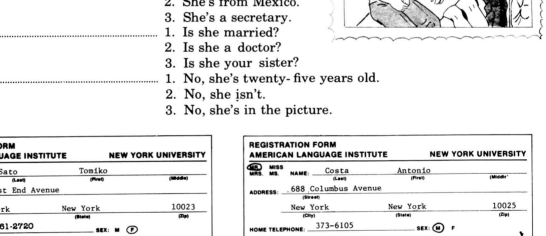

REGISTRATION FORM
AMERICAN LANGUAGE INSTITUTE   NEW YORK UNIVERSITY

MR. MISS
MRS. (MS.)   NAME: Sato   Tomiko
                   (Last)   (First)   (Middle)
ADDRESS: 270 West End Avenue
                   (Street)
New York   New York   10023
(City)   (State)   (Zip)
HOME TELEPHONE: 861-2720   SEX: M (F)
OCCUPATION: Secretary   DATE OF BIRTH: Oct. 10, 1970
                                        (Month) (Day) (Year)
PLACE OF BIRTH: Tokyo, Japan   COURSE: English 4
SIGNATURE: Tomiko Sato   DATE: Sept. 4, 1989

REGISTRATION FORM
AMERICAN LANGUAGE INSTITUTE   NEW YORK UNIVERSITY

(MR) MISS
MRS. MS.   NAME: Costa   Antonio
                 (Last)   (First)   (Middle)
ADDRESS: 688 Columbus Avenue
                 (Street)
New York   New York   10025
(City)   (State)   (Zip)
HOME TELEPHONE: 373-6105   SEX: (M) F
OCCUPATION: Restaurant employee DATE OF BIRTH: 3 15 69
                                               (Month) (Day) (Year)
PLACE OF BIRTH: Rio de Janeiro, Brazil COURSE: English 4
SIGNATURE: Antonio Costa   DATE: Sept. 3, 1989

REGISTRATION FORM
AMERICAN LANGUAGE INSTITUTE   NEW YORK UNIVERSITY

MR. MISS
MRS. (MS.)   NAME: Sanchez   Maria
                   (Last)   (First)   (Middle)
ADDRESS: 102 Bleecker Street
                   (Street)
New York   New York   10012
(City)   (State)   (Zip)
HOME TELEPHONE: 886-9785   SEX: M (F)
                student in hotel
OCCUPATION: administration   DATE OF BIRTH: 2 21 65
                                            (Month) (Day) (Year)
PLACE OF BIRTH: Mexico City, Mexico COURSE: English 4
SIGNATURE: Maria Sanchez   DATE: Sept. 3, 1989

Now answer the questions:

1. What's Tomiko's last name? ....
2. Where is Tony from? ....
3. What's Maria's telephone number? ....
4. Where's Tomiko from? ....
5. How old are Tony and Tomiko? ....
6. What's Tony's address? ....
7. What's Tomiko's telephone number? ....
8. How old is Maria? ....

Tomiko sees Tony in the Universi[ty] Coffee Shop.

Tomiko: Hi, Tony. How are you?
Tony: OK. And you?
Tomiko: I'm fine. Are those pictures? Can I see them?
Tony: Yes. Sit down.
Tomiko: Who's that?
Tony: My brother Nelson.
Tomiko: That's an unusual name. How do you spell it?
Tony: N-E-L-S-O-N. And that's his wife, Julia.
Tomiko: Oh, he's married? How old is he?
Tony: Twenty-seven. Are you married?
Tomiko: No, I'm not. Are you?
Tony: No. Do you have a boyfriend?
Tomiko: No.

Answer *That's right* or *That's wrong.*

1. Tomiko's married.
2. Julia's married.
3. Nelson's twenty-four.

Greet someone like this:

Tomiko: Hi, Tony. How are you?
Tony: OK. And you?
Tomiko: I'm fine.

A: Hi, ... How are you?
B: .... And you?
A: I'm ....

Ask about marital status. If someone is married, also ask if he/she has any children. If someone is single, ask if he/she has a boyfriend/girlfriend.

Tony: Are you married?
Tomiko: No, I'm not. Are you?
Tony: No. Do you have a boyfriend?
Tomiko: No.

A: Are you married?
B: .... Are you?
A: .... Do you have a boyfriend/ a girlfriend/any children?
B: ....

PRACTICE 12 Complete the conversation and practice it with a partner.

Karen: Who are they?
Sue: .... 1. Tony and Tomiko.
      2. They're tired.
      3. They're at the Institute.
Karen: .... 1. What are their names?
      2. What's his name?
      3. What do they do?
Sue: .... 1. They're sick.
      2. They're students
         at the Institute.
      3. They're married.
Karen: .... 1. Are they students
         at the Institute?
      2. Who are they?
      3. What course are
         they in?
Sue: .... 1. Yes.
      2. English 4.
      3. They're students.
Karen: .... 1. Are they in English 4?
      2. What do they do?
      3. Are they in Mr.
         Chapman's class?
Sue: .... 1. No, they're in Mr.
         Chapman's class.
      2. Yes.
      3. Here it is.

PRACTICE 13 This is a letter from Tomiko to her mother. There are eight sentences in the letter. Capitalize and punctuate the sentences.

September 30, 1989
Dear Mom,
      thanks for the newspaper article how are things at elizabeth eden im sure you're a fantastic director what does dad think
      im fine and i have some new friends they're all from different countries (egypt mexico italy japan and brazil) and they're very nice
      i miss you all write soon
                        Love
                        Tomiko

T R E A S U R E   H U N T

. . . FIND SOMEBODY WHO

1. is from _____ .
2. lives on your street.
3. has a phone number with four numbers that are in your phone number.
4. is a nurse.
5. has two brothers and one sister.
6. has a brother who is a doctor.
7. is married.
8. has a sister who is 18 years old.
9. has the same last name as your best friend.
10. has a girlfirend and her name is Gloria.

USEFUL LANGUAGE

. Where are you from?
. What do you do?
. How many brothers and sisters do you have?
. Do you have a brother? / Is your brother a doctor?
. Are you married?
. What's your last name?

Is there a bank near here?

Ali meets a new student at the International Students' Residence.

EXCUSE ME, IS THERE A BANK NEAR HERE?

YES, THERE'S ONE ON FIFTH AVENUE.

WHAT ABOUT A BOOKSTORE?

THERE ARE TWO. ONE'S ON BROADWAY AND ONE'S ON THE CORNER OF WASHINGTON PLACE AND GREENE STREET.

SAY, DO YOU HAVE A MAP BY ANY CHANCE?

I THINK I HAVE ONE IN MY ROOM. COME IN....

YEAH, HERE IT IS. HERE'S FIFTH AVENUE AND HERE'S THE BANK.

Franco:	Excuse me, is there a bank near here?
Ali:	Yes, there's one on Fifth Avenue.
Franco:	What about a bookstore?
Ali:	There are two. One's on Broadway and one's on the corner of Washington Place and Greene Street. Are you new here?
Franco:	Yes. My name's Franco Rossetti.
Ali:	Nice to meet you, Franco. I'm Ali Helal. Are you a student at the American Language Institute?
Franco:	Yes. Are you?
Ali:	Uh-huh. What course are you in?
Franco:	English 4.
Ali:	Terrific. So am I.
Franco:	Say, do you have a map, by any chance?
Ali:	I think I have one in my room. Come in. . . . Yeah, here it is. Here's Fifth Avenue and here's the bank.

Answer *That's right* **or** *That's wrong.*

1. Franco asks Ali where the American Language Institute is.
2. Both Franco and Ali are in English 4.
3. Ali wants a map.
4. Ali has a map in his room.

Read the street signs like this:
Second Avenue and Twelfth Street

FIRST	SECOND	THIRD	FOURTH	FIFTH	SIXTH	SEVENTH	EIGHTH	NINTH	TENTH	ELEVENTH	TWELFTH	THIRTEENTH
1st	2nd	3rd	4th	5th	6th	7th	8th	9th	10th	11th	12th	13th

FOURTEENTH	FIFTEENTH	SIXTEENTH	SEVENTEENTH	EIGHTEENTH	NINETEENTH	TWENTIETH	TWENTY-FIRST
14th	15th	16th	17th	18th	19th	20th	21st

**Ask and say where places are
like this:**

Franco: Is there a bank near here?
Ali: Yes, there's one on Fifth Avenue.

A: Is there a/an .... near here?
B: Yes, there's one on .... *or*
      No, there isn't. *or* I don't know.

**Ask and say where places are
like this:**

Franco: Is there a bookstore near here?
Ali: There are two. One's on Broadway and one's on
             the corner of Washington Place and Greene Street.

A: Is there a/an .... near here?
B: (Yes,) there are two. One's on ....
      and one's on .... *or* No, there isn't.
      or I don't know.

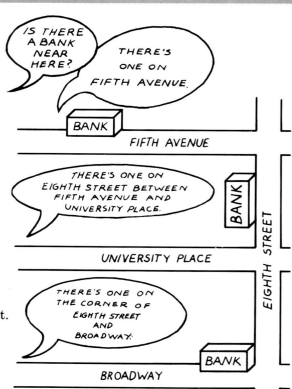

PRACTICE 4 Read this paragraph from the American Language Institute Bulletin and write *is* or *are*.

CONVENIENT LOCATION

New York University is conveniently located at Washington Square and students can get almost everything they need near the New York University campus. There .... a post office on 9th Street and there .... banks on Fifth Avenue, 8th Street and Broadway. There .... a bookstore on the corner of Washington Place and Greene Street and there .... also one on Broadway. There .... two drugstores and a supermarket on 8th Street. There .... many restaurants, coffee shops and movie theaters near the campus too.

PRACTICE 5 Show someone a map of your city or neighborhood.

Tony: Here's my apartment building. There's a post office here on 96th Street. There's a bank here.

A: Here's my ....
There's a/an .... here (on ....).

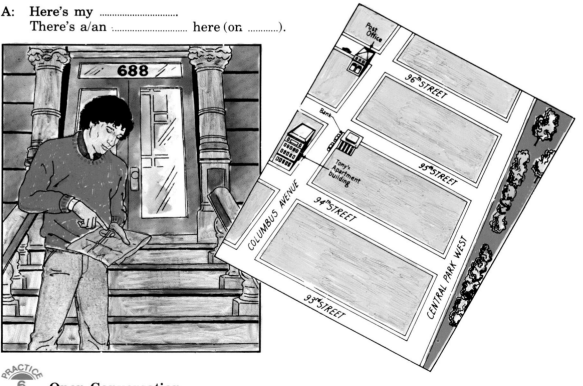

PRACTICE 6 Open Conversation

A: Excuse me, is there a/an .... near here?
B: Yes/No, ...
A: And is there a/an ....?
B· Yes/No, ...

49

EXPANSION

STUDYING AT THE AMERICAN LANGUAGE INSTITUTE

New York University is on Washington Square Park in historic Greenwich Village. There are more than 32,000 students at New York University. At least 5,000 are foreign students from 100 different countries.

The American Language Institute is part of New York University. It is on the corner of University Place and Washington Square North. The American Language Institute has English courses for foreign students, business-men and women, professionals, residents and tourists. There are both day and evening programs. The day program is nine hours a week and the evening program is six hours a week. There are classes for beginning, intermediate and advanced students, and there are also special classes in reading, writing, pronunciation and business English.

Students outside the United States can write to the American Language Institute, 1 Washington Square North, New York, New York 10003 for an application. The American Language Institute can also send you an I-20 form for a student visa.

Read the page from the American Language Institute Bulletin. Then circle the correct answers.

1. *At least* in "*At least* 5,000 are foreign students" means
   a) not 5,000.
   b) 5,000 or more.
2. *Historic* in "in *historic* Greenwich Village" means
   a) old.
   b) new.
3. *Foreign students* in "5,000 are *foreign students*" means
   a) students from the United States.
   b) students not from the United States.
4. *Outside* in "Students *outside* the United States" means
   a) not in the United States.
   b) in the United States.

Choose the correct word(s) and complete this paragraph with information about The Foreign Language Institute.

* 3,000
* writing and business English
* Michigan Avenue
* The Foreign Language Institute
* students and professionals
* FLI
* six
* The FLI

.... is on .... There are more than .... students at .... There are English courses for .... The .... has English courses ....days a week. There are also special courses in ....

 Listen for the information and complete the sentences.

1. There's a bank on .... Avenue.
2. There's a drugstore on .... Street between .... Avenue and .... Avenue.
3. Brentano's is on the corner of .... Street and .... Place.

"Is there a bank near here?"

HOW MUCH DO YOU KNOW?

1. Complete the Conversation

Franco: ....?
Ali: Yes, there's one on ....
Franco: ....?
Ali: No, there isn't. Are you new here?
Franco: ....
Ali: I'm new here too. I'm ....
Franco: My name's ....
Ali: ....
Franco: Nice to meet you too.

2. Find the Conversations

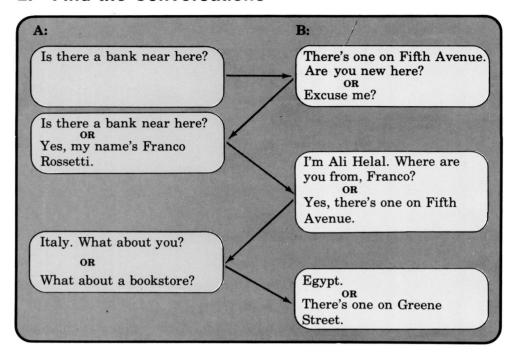

A:

Is there a bank near here?

Is there a bank near here?
OR
Yes, my name's Franco Rossetti.

Italy. What about you?
OR
What about a bookstore?

B:

There's one on Fifth Avenue. Are you new here?
OR
Excuse me?

I'm Ali Helal. Where are you from, Franco?
OR
Yes, there's one on Fifth Avenue.

Egypt.
OR
There's one on Greene Street.

3. Look at the map. Circle the answers.

1. The Chase Manhattan Bank is
   a) on 9th Street.
   b) on the corner of Fifth Avenue and 8th Street.
   c) between Broadway and University Place.
2. The University Coffee Shop is
   a) on the corner of 8th Street and Waverly Place.
   b) between 8th Street and 9th Street.
   c) on the corner of 8th Street and University Place.
3. There's a bookstore
   a) between 4th Street and Washington Place.
   b) between Washington Place and Waverly Place.
   c) on the corner of Washington Place and Greene Street.
4. There's a movie theater
   a) on the corner of 8th Street and University Place.
   b) on 8th Street between University Place and Broadway.
   c) on the corner of 8th Street and Fifth Avenue.

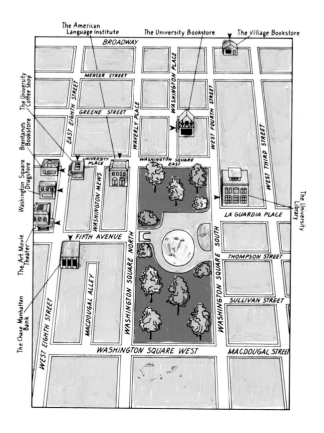

LANGUAGE SUMMARY

Now You Can Do This:

ask for locations: Is there a bank near here?

give locations: There's one on Fifth Avenue.
There are two. One's on Broadway and one's on the corner of Fifth Avenue and 8th Street.
Here's Fifth Avenue.

Grammar

There is/There are

Is there a drugstore near here?	Yes, **there's** one on Greene Street. Yes, **there are** two.

Prepositions: Location

The bookstore is **on the corner of** Washington Place and Greene Street.

The bookstore is **on** Broadway.

The drugstore is **near** the International Students' Residence.

The supermarket is **on** 8th Street, **between** University Place and Broadway.

Useful Words and Expressions

apartment building
place
avenue
street
bank
bookstore
corner
post office
drugstore
supermarket
restaurant
coffee shop
movie theater
park
•

new
•
near
on
between
•
What about you?
•

First, second, third,
fourth, fifth, sixth,
seventh, eighth,
ninth, tenth, eleventh,
twelfth, thirteenth,
fourteenth, fifteenth,
sixteenth, seventeenth,
eighteenth, nineteenth,
twentieth, twenty-first.

Where's Room 306?

Franco is in Ali's room.

Franco: Where can I buy a map like this?

Ali: You can get one at the University Bookstore.

Franco: Where's that?

Ali: On the corner of Washington Place and Greene Street.

Franco: Thanks a lot for your help, Ali. Oh, by the way, what time is class tonight?

Ali: It's at 7:00. I can't remember the room number, but you can ask in the office.

Franco: OK. Thanks again.

Ali: Any time. See you tonight.

Franco: Excuse me, miss.

Sue: Yes, can I help you?

Franco: Yes. Where's English 4?

Sue: It's in Room 306. That's on the third floor across from the Director's Office.

Franco: Thank you. Oh, and where's the men's room?

Sue: It's right there next to the elevator.

Franco: Thank you very much.

Sue: You're welcome.

Answer *That's right* **or** *That's wrong.*

1. Franco wants a map.
2. Ali knows English 4 is in Room 306.
3. English 4 is on the third floor.
4. The men's room is on the third floor.

Help someone find places on the map.
Ask and answer like this:

Sue: Can I help you?
Franco: Where's the University Bookstore?
Sue: It's on the corner of Washington Place and Greene Street.

A: Can I help you?
B: Where's the ....?
A: It's on .... *or* It's right here.

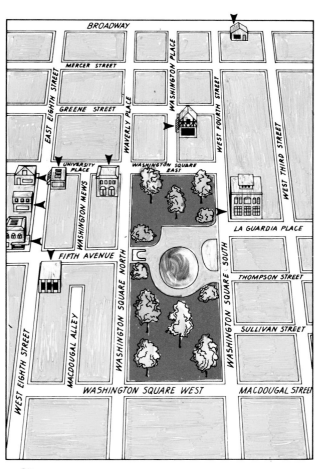

Find these places. (You can use the map on page 47 to find the correct locations.)

1. The University Bookstore
2. The Art Movie Theater
3. The University Library
4. The American Language Institute
5. The Chase Manhattan Bank
6. Brentano's Bookstore
7. The University Coffee Shop
8. Washington Square Drugstore

 Ask someone where you can buy something.
Tell someone where he/she can buy something.

Franco: Where can I buy a map?
Ali: At the University Bookstore.

A: Where can I buy a/some ....?
B: At ....
    **If you don't know the place,
    you can continue like this:**
A: Where's that?
B: It's on ....

NOTE:	
a map	(some) maps
a book	(some) books
a notebook	(some) notebooks
a sweater	(some) sweaters
BUT:	
(some) toothpaste	
(some) film	
(some) deodorant	

PRACTICE 3 Ask and say where places are like this:

Franco: Where's the men's room?
Sue: It's right there next to
         the elevator.

A: Where's ....?
B: (It's) ....

<table>
<tr><td>

NOTE:

Where's **the** library?
Where's **the** auditorium?
Where's **the** men's room?
Where's **the** ladies' room?
Where's **the** office?

BUT:

Where's Room 306?
</td></tr>
</table>

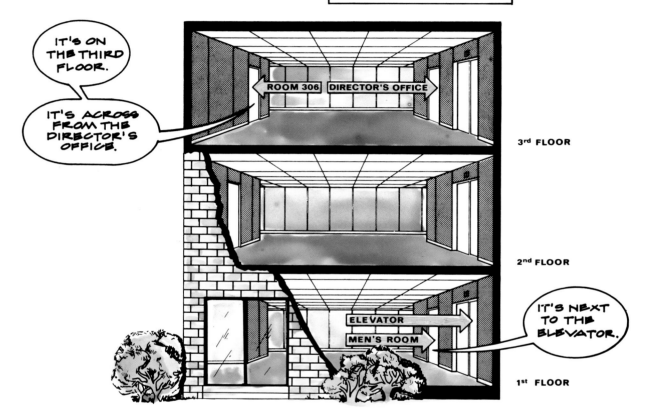

PRACTICE 4 Franco is asking Sue where places are. Write *there* or *it*.

Franco: Excuse me, where's Room 306?
Sue: ....'s on the third floor across
         from the Director's Office.
Franco: And where's the men's room?
Sue: ....'s a men's room next to
         the elevator and ....'s one on
         the third floor near the Director's Office.
Franco: Is .... a drinking fountain
         on this floor?
Sue: Yes, ...'s near the men's room.
Franco: And where's the library? Is .... on
         this floor too?
Sue: Yes. ....'s next to the auditorium.

PRACTICE 5 Open Conversation

A: Can I help you?
B: Yes, where can I ....?
A: At ....
B: Where's that?
A: On ....
B: And is there ....
    near here?
A: ....

EXPANSION

the *Waverly* bookstore
739 Broadway

AMERICAN COLLEGE DICTIONARY
$15.90 now $12.90

Used Books
Excellent Prices

POCKET CALCULATORS
$24.95 now $19.95

NOTEBOOKS
$1.50 now $1.20

This Week Only

10% Discount with Student Identification Cards
on all school and art supplies.

Open from 9 A.M. to 6 P.M. — Mondays and Thursdays until 9 P.M.

save at **REED'S** DRUGSTORE
Corner Sixth Avenue and 8th Street
Telephone 572-9083

DEODORANT
89¢
$1.25

TOOTHPASTE
79¢
89¢

RAZOR BLADES
$1.39
$1.59

SHAMPOO
$1.39
$1.59

PENS
49¢

SPECIAL SALE
Film and Cameras

Back-to-School **Sale**

ALL MERCHANDISE
20% off

● Women's Coats
● Sweaters
● Pants
● Slacks
● Dresses
● Men's Shoes
● Skirts
● Men's Shirts

Bennet's DEPARTMENT STORE
8th Street between
Fifth and Sixth Avenue

Open 9 A.M.—6 P.M.

Look at the advertisements and complete the sentences.

1. In advertisement 1 *Used* means   a) old.   b) new.
2. In advertisement 2 there is a *special sale* on   a) film and cameras.   b) maps.
3. In advertisement 2 *shampoo* is   a) $1.59.   b) $1.39.
4. In advertisement 3 a $100.00 coat on sale is   a) $100.00.   b) $80.00.

Look at the advertisements on page 57 and complete Sue's note to her husband.

NOTES

Ed –

I have a doctor's appointment this afternoon and I don't have time to go to the store before work. Could you please get me some toothpaste, deodorant and shampoo? You can get them at _____. It's on _____. Also, if you have time, there's a sale at _____. It's on _____. Maybe you can get the shirts you need. Men's shoes are on sale too. There's $20.00 on the refrigerator, if you need it. See you after work.

Love,

Sue

 Listen to the radio commercial and circle the answers.

1. You can buy   a) shoes   at the store.
                  b) school supplies
                  c) shampoo
2. The store is on   a) Wanamaker Place and Broadway.
                     b) Washington Place and Broadway.
                     c) Waverly Place and Broadway.
3. The advertisement is about a   a) bookstore.
                                  b) drugstore.
                                  c) department store.

HOW MUCH DO YOU KNOW?

1. Complete the Conversation

Sue: Can I help you?
Franco: ....?
Sue: At ....
Franco: Where's ....?
Sue: ....
Franco: And is there a .... near here?
Sue: .... Are you new here?
Franco: Yes. I'm a student at New York
          University.
Sue: ....?
Franco: Italy.

2. Find the Conversations

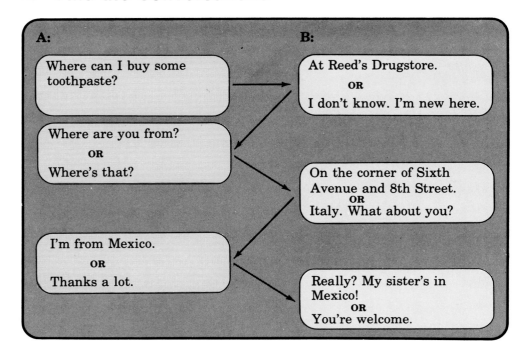

A:

Where can I buy some toothpaste?

Where are you from?
OR
Where's that?

I'm from Mexico.
OR
Thanks a lot.

B:

At Reed's Drugstore.
OR
I don't know. I'm new here.

On the corner of Sixth Avenue and 8th Street.
OR
Italy. What about you?

Really? My sister's in Mexico!
OR
You're welcome.

3. Circle the Answer

1. Can I help you?
   a) What about you?
   b) Me too.
   c) Yes. Where's Room 306?

2. Where can I buy a map?
   a) Yes, you can.
   b) Thank you.
   c) At the bookstore.

3. Where's Reed's Drugstore?
   a) It's near the drugstore.
   b) It's next to the drugstore.
   c) It's on Sixth Avenue.

4. Is there a bank near here?
   a) Yes. There's one near the Art Movie Theater.
   b) Yes, it's near here.
   c) No, it isn't near here.

5. Where is the men's room?
   a) Next to the bank.
   b) Next to the movie theater.
   c) Next to the telephones.

LANGUAGE SUMMARY

Now You Can Do This:

offer to help someone:	Can I help you?
ask for locations:	Where's the bookstore? Where's that? Where can I buy a map?
give locations:	On 8th Street. At the University Bookstore.
thank people:	Thank you.
accept thanks:	You're welcome.

Grammar

Prepositions: Location

Where can I buy a map?		**At** the University Bookstore.
Where's Room 306?	It's	**on** the third floor. **next to** the elevator. **across from** the Director's Office. **near** the Director's Office.

The

Where's	**the**	library? men's room?
		Room 306?

Count Nouns		Mass Nouns
a map	(some) maps	(some) toothpaste
a book	(some) books	(some) film
a notebook	(some) notebooks	(some) deodorant
a sweater	(some) sweaters	

Useful Words and Expressions

can	coffee shop	elevator	some	Thanks a lot.
buy (v)	drugstore	*drinking fountain*	•	You're welcome.
help (v)	institute	map	right here	
•	university	toothpaste	right there	
	third floor	•	•	
	auditorium		at	
	Director's Office		next to	
	ladies' room		in	
	men's room		*across from*	
	library		•	

Let's get something to eat.

Tomiko, Franco and Tony are in Mr. Chapman's class.

Mr. Chapman:	Tomiko, what time is it, please?
Tomiko:	It's 8:30.
Mr. Chapman:	Already? Well, I guess that's all for tonight. See you tomorrow.
Franco:	Let's get something to eat. I'm really hungry.
Tony:	That's a good idea. There's a coffee shop near here. Let's go there.
Franco:	Is it expensive?
Tony:	No, it's really cheap. You can get a hamburger for 95 cents.
Tomiko:	Yes. but the food isn't very good.
Tony:	That's true. Well then, where can we get something to eat?
Tomiko:	What about Amy's Restaurant?
Tony:	Oh, yeah. We can go there. Can you go with us, Mr. Chapman?
Mr. Chapman:	I'm sorry, I can't. I have to do some work. Maybe next time.
Tomiko:	I really can't go either.
Tony:	Oh? Why not?
Tomiko:	I'm tired and I have to study.
Tony:	Come on, just for a little while.
Tomiko:	Well, OK, but I can't stay long.

Answer *That's right* **or** *That's wrong.*

1. The coffee shop has good food.
2. Mr. Chapman goes to Amy's restaurant.
3. Tomiko goes to the restaurant with Franco and Tony.

Ask someone what time it is. Tell someone the time.

Mr. Chapman: What time is it, please?
Tomiko: It's 8:30.

A: What time is it, (please)?
B: ....

| 4:00 | 5:15 | 6:30 | 7:45 | 8:00 |
| **(four o'clock)** | **(five fifteen)** | **(six thirty)** | **(seven forty-five)** | **(eight o'clock)** |

 Suggest getting something to eat/drink. Accept or say you can't accept like this:

Tony: Let's get something to eat.
Mr. Chapman: I'm sorry, I can't.

A: Let's get something to ....
B: I'm sorry, I can't. *or* That's a good idea.

 **Ask someone where you can get something to eat/drink.
Tell someone where he/she can get something to eat/drink.**

Franco: Where can I get something to eat?
Tony: There's a coffee shop near here.

A: Where can I/we get something to ....?
B: There's a .... on/near ....

You Can Also Say:
At **Amy's Restaurant.**
At **the University Coffee Shop.**

Suggest going somewhere.
4 **Say why you can't go somewhere.**

Tony: Let's go to the University Coffee Shop.
Tomiko: I'm sorry, I can't.
Tony: Why not?
Tomiko: I have to meet someone.

A: Let's go ....
B: I'm sorry, I can't.
A: Why not?
B: I have to ....

<table>
<tr><td>NOTE:</td></tr>
</table>

NOTE:

the University Coffee Shop
the Greenwich Restaurant
the movies
the theater

BUT:
McDonald's
Jane's Coffee Shop
Amy's Restaurant

 Franco, Maria, Ali and Jeannette are talking. Write *can,*
5 *can't,* **or** *have to* **with the words in parentheses.**

Franco: What about you, Maria? Ali? Let's get something to eat.
Maria: I .... home. It's already 8:45, and I ....
                   (go)   (study)
Ali: I'm sorry, I .... either. I .... my homework.
                                        (go)   (do)
Jeannette: I .... my husband at 9:30, but I .... for a
                   (meet)   (stay)
            little while.

 Open Conversation
6

A: What time is it?
B: ....
A: Where can we get something to eat?
B: At ....
A: Where is it?
B: ....
A: OK. Let's go.

EXPANSION

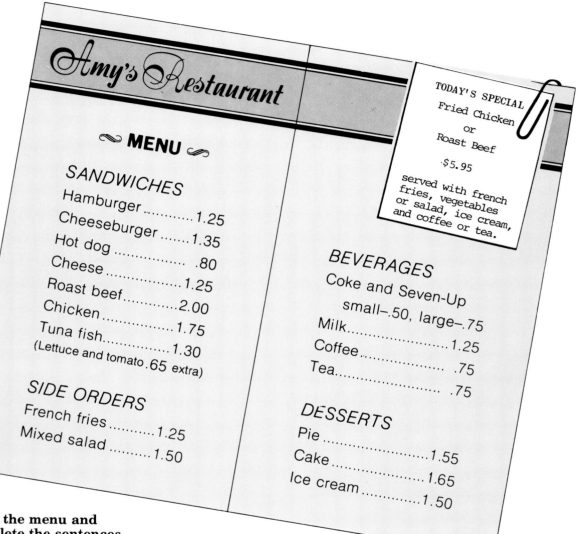

Amy's Restaurant

～ MENU ～

SANDWICHES
Hamburger 1.25
Cheeseburger 1.35
Hot dog .... .80
Cheese 1.25
Roast beef 2.00
Chicken 1.75
Tuna fish 1.30
(Lettuce and tomato .65 extra)

SIDE ORDERS
French fries 1.25
Mixed salad 1.50

TODAY'S SPECIAL
Fried Chicken
or
Roast Beef
$5.95
served with french
fries, vegetables
or salad, ice cream,
and coffee or tea.

BEVERAGES
Coke and Seven-Up
small–.50, large–.75
Milk 1.25
Coffee .... .75
Tea .... .75

DESSERTS
Pie ....
Cake 1.55
Ice cream 1.65
                       1.50

Read the menu and complete the sentences.

1. A chicken sandwich
   is $................. .
2. Today's specials
   are ....
   and ....
3. Specials are served
   with ....
   and ....
   or ....
4. There are ....
   and .... Cokes.
5. Cheeseburgers are
   $................. .

Read this note from Jim Chapman. Then write a note to a friend. Ask him/her to get you something to eat.

SUE,
I HAVE TO WORK LATE TONIGHT.
COULD YOU GET ME SOMETHING TO
EAT WHEN YOU GO OUT FOR DINNER?
I'D LIKE A HAMBURGER WITH LETTUCE
AND TOMATO, AND AN ORDER OF FRENCH
FRIES. HERE'S $10.00. THANKS A LOT.

JIM

P.S. PLEASE GET ME A LARGE COKE
TOO.

—————————,
I have to—————————.
Could you get me something
to eat when you go out for
—————————?I'd like
—————————
Here's ———. Thanks a lot.

—————————

 Listen and complete the sentences.

1. Tony's watch says ....
2. Tomiko's watch says ....
3. Franco's watch says ....

HOW MUCH DO YOU KNOW?

1. Complete the Conversation

Tony:	....?
Tomiko:	8:30.
Tony:	....?
Tomiko:	At Amy's Restaurant.
Tony:	....?
Tomiko:	On Greene Street.
Tony:	....?
Tomiko:	No, it's cheap.
Tony:	Can you go with me?
Tomiko:	....
Tony:	Why not?
Tomiko:	....
Tony:	Oh, come on. Just for a little while.
Tomiko:	....

2. Find the Conversations

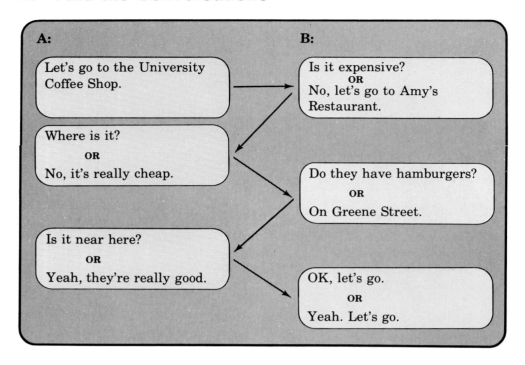

A:

Let's go to the University Coffee Shop.

Where is it?

OR

No, it's really cheap.

Is it near here?

OR

Yeah, they're really good.

B:

Is it expensive?

OR

No, let's go to Amy's Restaurant.

Do they have hamburgers?

OR

On Greene Street.

OK, let's go.

OR

Yeah. Let's go.

3. Circle the Answer

1. Let's get something to eat.
   a) Coffee, please.
   b) No, I'm hungry.
   c) That's a good idea.

2. Is the coffee shop on Fifth Avenue?
   a) No, I can't stay long.
   b) No, it's on 3rd Avenue.
   c) They have hamburgers.

3. I'm sorry. I can't go.
   a) That's a good idea.
   b) Why not?
   c) What time?

4. I'm really hungry.
   a) I can't.
   b) That's a good idea.
   c) Let's go to Amy's.

5. Why not?
   a) That's a good idea.
   b) I have to study.
   c) OK.

LANGUAGE SUMMARY

Now You Can Do This:

ask the time:	What time is it, (please)?
tell someone the time:	It's 8:30.
make a suggestion:	Let's get something to eat.
accept a suggestion:	OK, let's go. That's a good idea.
say you can't do something:	I'm sorry, I can't. I have to meet someone.

Grammar

Information Questions ⟶ And Answers

What time	is it?		8:25.
Where	is it?		At Amy's.
	can I	get something to eat?	On 3rd Street.

Have to/Has to

I We You They	**have to**	meet a friend. study.
He She	**has to**	go home.

Useful Words and Expressions

can't
get (v)
go (v)
have to
let's
eat (v)
•
hamburgers
idea
restaurant
time
•

someone
something
we
•
cheap
good
expensive
•
really
yeah
•

why
•
but
•
What time is it?
Why not?
Please.
Thank you.
Let's go.
That's a good idea.
eight thirty

What would you like?

Tony, Tomiko and Franco are at Amy's Restaurant.

Waitress:	Are you ready to order?
Tony:	Yes, I think so. I'd like a hamburger with lettuce and tomato, and a glass of milk.
Waitress:	How would you like your hamburger?
Tony:	Medium.
Franco:	The same for me, and could I have some french fries with that?
Waitress:	Sure. And what would you like, miss?
Tomiko:	Just coffee, please.
Waitress:	Is that all?
Tomiko:	Yes, I think so.

Tony:	Excuse me, miss. How much is a piece of pie?
Waitress:	$1.55.
Tony:	What kind do you have?
Waitress:	Chocolate, lemon and apple.
Tony:	I'd like apple, please.
Waitress:	Would anybody else like dessert?
Tomiko:	No, thank you. Just more coffee, please.
Waitress:	Sure.
Franco:	And could I have my check? I have to go.

Answer *That's right* **or** *That's wrong.*

1. Tony isn't ready to order.
2. Tomiko is hungry.
3. Franco would like a hamburger with lettuce and tomato.
4. Franco likes potatoes.

NOTE:

(some) salt	**BUT:** a sandwich
(some) sugar	a **piece** of cake
(some) coffee	a **cup** of coffee
(some) water	a **glass** of water
(some) milk	a **glass** of milk

1 **Ask someone if he/she is ready to order. Give someone your order.**

Waitress: Are you ready to order?
Tony: Yes. I'd like a hamburger with lettuce and tomato, and a glass of milk.

A: Are you ready to order?
B: Yes. I'd like .... *or* No, not yet.

2 **Ask someone what he/she wants to eat/drink.**
Tell someone what you want to eat/drink.

Waitress: What would you like?
Franco: I'd like some french fries.

A: What would you like?
B: I'd like ....

You can continue like this:

A: Is that all?
B: Yes, I think so. *or* No, I'd like .... too.

"*I'd like a chicken sandwich, a piece of apple pie, the special of the day, french fries, a salad, a hamburger with lettuce and tomato, a piece of cake . . .*"

3 **Talk about food. Ask what kind there is. Say what kind you want.**

Tony: What kind of pie do you have?
Waitress: Chocolate and apple.
Tony: Apple, please.

A: What kind of .... do you have?
B: .... and ....
A: ...., please.

4 **You can also ask for things like this:**

Franco: Could I have some french fries?
Waitress: Sure.

A: ....?
B: Sure. *or* I'm sorry we don't have ....

You Can Also Say:

Franco: More coffee, please.
Waitress: Of course.
Franco: Some sugar, please.
Waitress: Certainly.
Franco: Check, please.
Waitress: Yes, sir / ma'am / miss.

Sue is ordering something to eat. She is also ordering something to take to Jim Chapman. Write *a* **or** *some*.

Waitress: Can I help you?
Sue: Yes. I'd like .... chicken sandwich, ...
french fries and .... cup of coffee, please. Oh, and
.... ice cream. What kind do you have?
Waitress: Vanilla, chocolate and strawberry.
Sue: .... small dish of chocolate, please.
Waitress: Is that all?
Sue: No. I'd also like .... hamburger with lettuce and
tomato, ... french fries, and .... large Coke to
go.
Waitress: Sure.

 Open Conversation

A: Are you ready to order?
B: Yes. I'd like ....
A: Sure.
B: And what kind of ....?
A: ....
B: ...., please.
A: Is that all?
B: ....

EXPANSION

**Read the paragraphs. In each paragraph there's one sentence that
does not refer to the subject of the paragraph. Cross out the
sentence. Look at the example in the first paragraph.**

AROUND GREENWICH VILLAGE

By ANN ROCHETTE

There are many good restaurants and coffee shops in Greenwich Village where you can get everything from a snack to a complete meal. ~~There are good bookstores in Greenwich Village too.~~ These small, informal restaurants are inexpensive and they usually have good service.

Amy's Restaurant is an example of a good place to eat in Greenwich Village. It's located on Greene Street near New York University. Jim Chapman teaches at New York University. Amy's is a perfect place for students to eat lunch and dinner. It's clean, the service is fast and the prices are reasonable.

Amy's has a different special every day. The special includes fish or meat, vegetables, a mixed salad, bread and butter, dessert, and coffee or tea—all for $5.95. The special and the other items on Amy's menu are always excellent for the price. The prices are good at the Waverly Bookstore too.

Franco has to pay for a hamburger with lettuce and tomato, a glass of milk and some french fries. Complete this check for Franco.

Amy's Restaurant
GUEST CHECK

DATE | SERVER NO. | PERSONS | GUEST CHECK NO.
40550

1 burger l+T
1 f.f.
1 milk

8% TAX

RC 36 · THANK YOU

Ask and answer like this. (One person can look at the menu on page 64.)

Franco: How much is a hamburger with lettuce and tomato?

Waitress: $3.60 (three-sixty).

A: How much is/are ....?
B: $.. .

Sue is ordering something to eat, but she can't get everything she wants. Listen and write the things she gets.

_____

_____

_____

~MENU~

Today's SPECIAL : Chicken Sandwich and Vegetable Soup $3.75

SANDWICHES
Tuna fish $ 2.25
Hamburger $ 2.95
Cheeseburger $ 3.50
Lettuce and tomato extra .65

SIDE ORDERS
French fries 1.25
Mixed salad 1.50

BEVERAGES
Coke .75
Coffee .75
Tea .75

HOW MUCH DO YOU KNOW?

1. Complete the Conversation

Waitress:	....?
Tony:	Yes, I'd like a hamburger.
Waitress:	With lettuce and tomato?
Tony:	Yes, and .... too.
Waitress:	Would you like dessert?
Tony:	Yes, what kind of ....?
Waitress:	....
Tony:	I'd like ....
Waitress:	.... all?
Tony:	I'd like .... too.

2. Find the Conversations

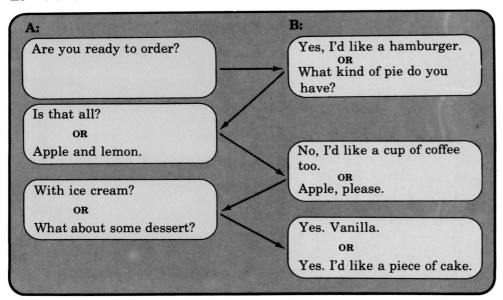

A:

> Are you ready to order?

> Is that all?
>
> **OR**
>
> Apple and lemon.

> With ice cream?
>
> **OR**
>
> What about some dessert?

B:

> Yes, I'd like a hamburger.
>
> **OR**
>
> What kind of pie do you have?

> No, I'd like a cup of coffee too.
>
> **OR**
>
> Apple, please.

> Yes. Vanilla.
>
> **OR**
>
> Yes. I'd like a piece of cake.

3. Circle the Answer

1. Are you ready to order?
   a) What would you like?
   b) Is that all?
   c) No, not yet.

2. What would you like?
   a) At Amy's.
   b) A hamburger.
   c) Tony and Tomiko.

3. What kind of ice cream do you have?
   a) Yes, I'd like some.
   b) Yes, we have some.
   c) Chocolate and vanilla.

4. Is that all?
   a) No, that's all.
   b) Really?
   c) Yes, I think so.

5. Can I have my check, please?
   a) With ice cream?
   b) I have to meet a friend.
   c) Sure.

LANGUAGE SUMMARY

Now You Can Do This:

take an order:
Are you ready to order?
What would you like?
Is that all?

order something to eat:
I'd like a hamburger with lettuce and tomato.
What kind of pie do you have?
Apple pie, please.
Could I have some french fries?

ask for prices:
How much is a piece of pie?

Grammar

Would

What **would** you like?
I'**d** like a hamburger.

Mass Nouns	Count Nouns
(some) salt	a sandwich
(some) sugar	a **piece** of cake
(some) coffee	a **cup** of coffee
(some) water	a **glass** of water
(some) milk	a **glass** of milk

Useful Words and Expressions

could	lemon pie	ma'am	what kind of
'd (would)	vanilla ice cream	miss	how about
like (**v**)	french fries	sir	how much
order (**v**)	lettuce	•	•
would	tomato	all	with
•	coffee	ready	•
dessert	milk	•	Not yet.
cake	piece	so	Is that all?
apple pie	glass	yet	I think so.
chocolate pie	cup	•	Sure.

What do you do in your free time?

Tomiko has to go home.

Tomiko: **What time do you have?**

Tony: **It's 10:15.**

Tomiko: **Oh, I have to go. I live with my cousin and his wife, and they worry about me.**

Tony: **Where do you live?**

Tomiko: **On West End Avenue near 72nd Street.**

Tony: **We can take the subway together. I live on Columbus Avenue and 94th Street.**

Tomiko: **Who do you live with?**

Tony: **I live alone.**

Tomiko: **Don't you ever get lonely?**

Tony: **Sometimes, but not very often. And I really don't have time to get lonely. I work every day except Sunday and I go to school at night. Do you just study, or do you work too?**

Tomiko: **I work for Japan Air Lines.**

Tony: **Oh, that's right. So you're pretty busy too.**

Tomiko: **Not really. I only work part time.**

Tony: **And what do you do in your free time?**

Tomiko: **Oh, read, help around the house, watch TV. . . .**

Answer *That's right* **or** *That's wrong.*

1. Tomiko lives alone.
2. Tomiko is very busy.
3. Tony is very lonely.
4. *Part time* means "not all day."

1   **Ask someone where he/she lives. Tell someone where you live.**

Tony: Where do you live?
Tomiko: On West End Avenue near 72nd Street.

A: Where do you live?
B: On ....

You Can Say:
I live
on West End Avenue.
at 270 West End Avenue.
in New York.

2   **Ask someone who he/she lives with. Tell someone who you live with.**

Tomiko: Who do you live with?
Tony: I live alone.

A: Who do you live with?
B: I live alone. *or* I live with ....

If someone lives alone, you can continue like this:

A: Don't you ever get lonely?
B: Sometimes. *or* No, not usually.

3   **Ask if someone works or just studies. Say what you do.**

Tony: Do you just study, or do you work too?
Tomiko: I work for Japan Air Lines.

A: Do you just study, or do you work too?
B: I work for .... *or* I'm a/an ....
      or I just study.

4   **Ask someone what he/she does in his/her free time.**
Tell someone what you do in your free time.

Tony: What do you do in your free time?
Tomiko: Oh, read, help around the house, watch TV. . . .

A: What do you do in your free time?
B: ....

"What do you do in your free time?"

PRACTICE 5 Tony and Tomiko are talking in the subway station.
Write *do*, *is*, or *'s*.

Tony: Where .... you live?
Tomiko: On West End Avenue.
Tony: I have some friends on West End Avenue. What .... your address?
Tomiko: 270 West End Avenue.
Tony: They live at 224. .... you live alone?
Tomiko: No. I live with my cousin, Toshi, and his wife.
Tony: What .... you do in your free time?
Tomiko: I watch TV and sometimes I go to the movies.
Tony: .... there a movie theater near you?
Tomiko: Yeah, there .... one on 72nd Street.
Tony: Let's go to a movie sometime.
Tomiko: That .... a good idea.

PRACTICE 6 Open Conversation

A: Where do you live?
B: ....
A: Who do you live with?
B: ....
A: Do you just study, or do you work too?
B: ....
A: What do you do in your free time?
B: ....

EXPANSION

NEW YORK NEWS

What do you think?

by Roberta Davis

(1) Many people in the United States live alone. (2) Some live alone because they like to be independent, and others live alone because they don't have anyone to live with.

(3) Young people leave home after high school and get jobs or go to college. (4) They leave home because they want to learn about themselves and experience life before they get married and have families.

(5) Older people often have to live alone. (6) Sometimes they don't have families. (7) Sometimes they are widows or widowers, and their children don't want to take care of them. (8) These people are often very lonely.

What Do People Think About Living Alone?

Nancy Zenakis, 15, student

(9) I certainly want to live alone when I finish high school. (10) I want to see what I can do myself. (11) If your family or your husband helps you all your life, you never learn about yourself.

Bob Carpenter, 26, bus driver

(12) Living alone is OK. (13) I don't want a roommate. (14) I'd like to get married someday, but I prefer to live alone until then.

Mary Webster, 69, retired store clerk

(15) I have three children, but I live alone. (16) Two of my children live in California and one lives in Texas, and I'm lucky if I see them at Christmas! (17) I'm lonely sometimes, but I have friends here in New York. (18) I don't want to live in California, but I'd like one of my children to come here and live with me.

 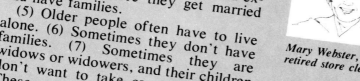

Read the newspaper article above and circle the correct answers.

1. In sentence (2) *others* refers to   a) other people.   b) other countries.
2. In sentence (4) *themselves* refers to   a) young people.   b) families.
3. In sentence (8) *these people* refers to   a) older people.   b) families.
4. In sentence (10) *myself* refers to   a) Nancy Zenakis.   b) family.
5. In sentence (14) *until then* refers to   a) until I get married.   b) until I find a roommate.

8 **Read the newspaper article and circle the correct answer.**

1. Some young people live alone because
   a) they don't have anyone to live with.
   b) they want to get married.
   c) they want to experience life.

2. Older people often live alone because
   a) they don't have families.
   b) they want to learn about themselves and experience life.
   c) they are very lonely.

3. Nancy Zenakis wants to live alone because
   a) she wants to be independent.
   b) she wants to finish high school.
   c) she wants to marry Bob Carpenter.

4. Mary Webster wants
   a) to live in California.
   b) to have friends in New York.
   c) one of her children to live with her in New York.

9 **Find the sentences that continue the idea of the paragraph. Write them and finish the paragraph.**

What Does Oscar Vega Think?

Oscar Vega, 29 Salesman

My father lives alone, but he's never lonely. He's busy all the time.

He's sick.
He has a lot of friends and they often go to the movies.
My aunt is lonely too.
He reads a lot and he loves to watch TV.
He doesn't like ice cream.
He also takes evening courses at New York University.
My brother is a student at New York University.

10 **Listen to the TV reporter and fill in the information.**

Mr. Snyder is from .... His mother lives
                  a) New York
                  b) Mexico
in .... and she lives ....
    a) New York   a) alone
    b) Florida   b) with her son
Mr. Snyder thinks it's .... for older people to live alone.
               a) terrible
               b) OK

HOW MUCH DO YOU KNOW?

1. Complete the Conversation

Tomiko: ....?
Tony: It's 10:30. Why?
Tomiko: I have to go home.
Tony: ....?
Tomiko: I live with my cousin and his wife.
Tony: ....?
Tomiko: He's a businessman.
Tony: ....?
Tomiko: I work and study.
Tony: Where ....?
Tomiko: I work for Japan Air Lines.

2. Find the Conversations

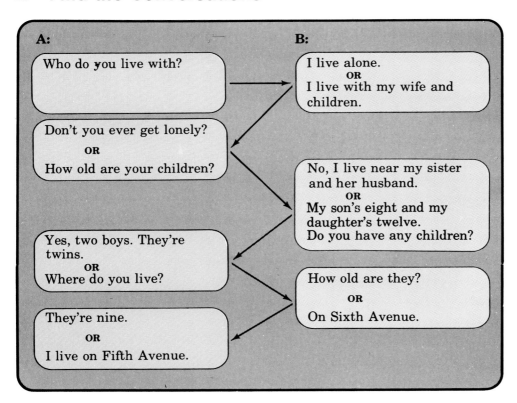

3. Circle the Answer

1. What time do you have?

    a) Yes, I do.
    b) Not yet.
    c) 9:45.

2. Who do you live with?

    a) On 82nd Street.
    b) I live with my cousin and his wife.
    c) Yes. I live with my parents.

3. Where do you live?

    a) On 3rd Avenue.
    b) Yes, I live there.
    c) No, I live alone.

4. What do you do in your free time?

    a) I'm a secretary.
    b) I read and watch TV.
    c) No, I don't.

5. Do you just study, or do you work too?

    a) Yes, I study.
    b) Yes, I work.
    c) I work for my uncle.

LANGUAGE SUMMARY

Now You Can Do This:

ask where someone lives:	Where do you live?
say where you live:	I live on West End Avenue.
	I live at 270 West End Avenue.
	I live in New York.
ask personal questions:	Who do you live with?
	Don't you ever get lonely?
	What do you do in your free time?

Grammar

Prepositions: Location

I live	**on** West End Avenue.
	at 270 West End Avenue.
	in New York.

Questions ⟶ And Answers

Who	**do**	you		live	with?
	Don't	you	ever	get	lonely?
	Do	you	just	study	or
	do	you		work	too?

I live alone.
Sometimes, but not very often.

I work for Japan Air Lines.

Useful Words and Expressions

live (**v**)	boys	sometimes
study (**v**)	twins	usually
work (**v**)	son	just
read (**v**)	daughter	•
watch (**v**)	•	or
•	alone	•
free time	lonely	for
house	•	around
TV	ever	

What kind of movies do you like?

Tomiko and Tony are on the subway. They're talking about things they like to do.

Tomiko: Do you like American TV?

Tony: It's OK, but I like movies better.

Tomiko: What kind of movies do you like?

Tony: All kinds, but especially westerns.

Tomiko: Who's your favorite actor?

Tony: Clint Eastwood.

Tomiko: Yeah, he's good. I like him too. How often do you go to the movies?

Tony: About once a month. Actually, I don't go very often because I don't like to go alone and I don't have many friends in New York.

Tomiko: I know what you mean. I'd like to play tennis more often too, but I can't find anyone to play with.

Tony: I play tennis.

Tomiko: You're kidding!

Tony: No. I play every morning before I go to work. Would you like to play sometime?

Tomiko: Sure. I'd love to— but maybe not so early.

Answer *That's right* **or** *That's wrong.*

1. Tomiko doesn't have many friends in New York
2. Tomiko thinks Clint Eastwood is a good actor.
3. Tony likes westerns.

PRACTICE 1 Ask someone what he/she likes.
Tell someone what you like.

Tomiko: Do you like American TV?
Tony: It's OK, but I like movies better.

A: Do you like ....?
B: It's/They're OK, but I like .... better. *or* Yes, I do. *or* No, I don't.

LIKES AND DISLIKES					
Do you like:	Yes	No	**Do you like:**	Yes	No
football?			to read?		
sports?			to dance?		
music?			to sing?		
movies?			to play baseball?		

PRACTICE 2 Ask someone what kind
of movies/books he/she likes.
Tell someone what kind
you like.

Tomiko: What kind of movies do you like?
Tony: All kinds, but especially westerns.

A: What kind of .... do
you like?
B: (I like) ....
or I don't really like movies.

NOTE:	
MOVIES	BOOKS
I like comed**ies**.	I like biograph**ies**.
musical**s**.	myster**ies**.
war mov**ies**.	love stor**ies**.
BUT:	
I like science fiction.	

MOVIES

Comedy

Science Fiction

BOOKS

Mystery

Love Story

Musical

Western

Autobiography

PRACTICE 3 Talk about music.

Tomiko: What kind of music do you like?
Tony: All kinds, but especially classical.

A: What kind of .... do you like?
B: (I like) ....

M. Giraudon
Classical

ABKCO Records, Inc.
Rock

Jazz

© 1976 by Polydor Inc.
Reprinted under license.

Disco

PRACTICE 4 Talk about favorite people.

Tomiko: Who's your favorite actor?
Tony: Clint Eastwood.

A: Who's your favorite ....?
B: ....

© 1978 by Columbia Pictures Inc.
Jane Fonda, *actress*

© 1975 by United Artists Corp.
All rights reserved.

Paul McCartney and
John Lennon, *composers*

From the motion picture *Smokey and the Bandit*
Courtesy of Universal Pictures

Burt Reynolds, *actor*

Pelé, *soccer player*

© 1978 by Columbia Pictures Inc.
Donna Summer, *singer*

Ernest Hemingway, *author*

5 Ask someone how often he/she does something.

NOTE:					
How often do you go	**to** the movies? **to** football games? **to** concerts?	**BUT:**	How often do you go		swimm**ing?** fish**ing?** danc**ing?**

Tomiko: How often do you go to the movies?
Tony: About once a month.

A: How often do you ....?
B: About .... *or* I never ....

You Can Also Say:			
Every	Monday Tuesday Wednesday Thursday Friday Saturday Sunday	**Once** **Twice**	a week a month a year
		Every	day week month

6 Invite someone to do something. Accept or refuse someone's invitation.

Tony: Would you like to play tennis sometime?
Tomiko: Sure. I'd love to.

A: Would you like to ....?
B: Sure. I'd love to. *or* I'm sorry, I can't.

You Can Also Say:
I'm sorry, I don't know **how.**

7 Tony and Tomiko are talking.
Write *do, 's* or *are.*

Tony: .... you like to read?
Tomiko: Yes, I ....
Tony: What kind of books .... you like?
Tomiko: Oh, all kinds, but especially science fiction.
Tony: Who .... your favorite author?
Tomiko: Isaac Asimov.
Tony: ....n't you like Bradbury?
Tomiko: Yes, I like him too. He and Asimov .... both very good.

8 Open Conversation

A: Do you like movies?
B: Yes, ...
A: What kind of ....?
B: ....
A: Who's your favorite ....?
B: ....

A: How often do you go ....?
B: ....
A: Would you like to ....?
B: ....

EXPANSION

September 30, 1989

Dear Akiko,

I love New York. It's a fabulous city and you can find everything you want here. There are movie theaters, museums, excellent restaurants and fantastic department stores and boutiques. Of course, New York is a very expensive city too – especially for a student with a part-time job.

Living in New York is exciting but my life is a little boring sometimes. Every day I get up at 8:30, have breakfast with Toshi and Lynn and go to work. At work I just type, answer the phone and type some more. Also, I don't have many friends at work, so I usually have lunch alone at a coffee shop. In the afternoon I go home and study or read. That's my day.

I have my English class in the evening. At least that's not boring. In fact, I really like it. I have an excellent teacher, and the other students are very nice – especially a guy from Brazil. His name's Tony and he plays tennis. I finally have someone to play tennis with.

I have to go now. I have to do my homework. Say hello to everybody for me and write soon.

Love
Tomiko

9 **Circle the correct answers.**

1. Paragraph 1 says
   a) Tomiko likes New York.
   b) Tomiko doesn't like New York.
   c) Tomiko wants a part-time job.

2. Paragraph 2 says
   a) Tomiko's life is exciting every day.
   b) Tomiko's life is a little boring.
   c) Tomiko's life is different every day.

3. Paragraph 3 says
   a) Tomiko likes her class.
   b) Tomiko doesn't like her class.
   c) Tony likes his class.

10 **Complete the letter below with your own information. Write about your daily activities. Include:** *1. the date 2. the opening 3. the closing 4. margins 5. indentation.*

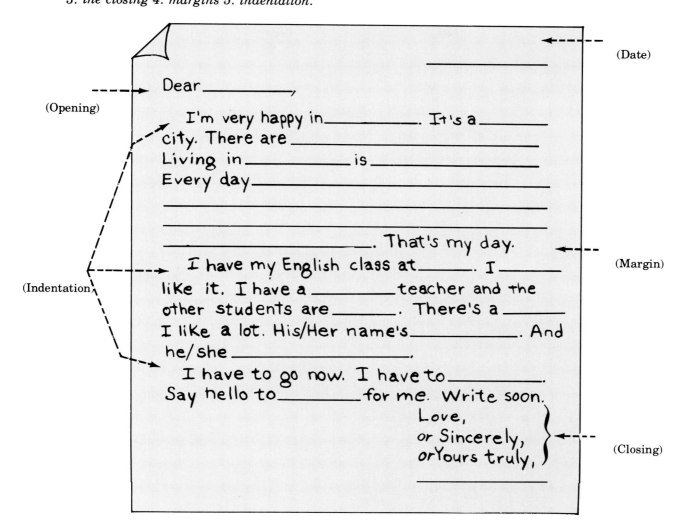

(Date)

(Opening)

Dear_____,

I'm very happy in_____. It's a_____
city. There are_____
Living in_____ is_____
Every day_____
_____
_____
_____. That's my day.

(Margin)

I have my English class at_____. I_____
like it. I have a_____ teacher and the
other students are_____. There's a_____
I like a lot. His/Her name's_____. And
he/she_____,

(Indentation)

I have to go now. I have to_____.
Say hello to_____ for me. Write soon.
          Love,
          or Sincerely,
          orYours truly,

(Closing)

11 **Jim Chapman meets Peggy Lewis and Ann Mitchell at a party. Peggy and Ann are both from Florida, but Peggy lives in New York now. Ann is in New York for a tennis tournament. Listen to the conversation and answer the questions.**

1. What does Jim do?
2. Where does he live now?
3. Where would he like to live?
4. What does he do in his free time?
5. Choose a girlfriend for Jim. Peggy or Ann? Why?

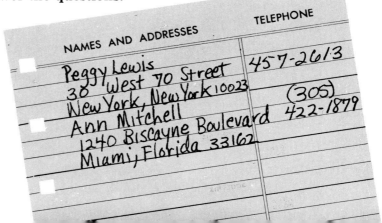

NAMES AND ADDRESSES   TELEPHONE

Peggy Lewis
30 West 70 Street   457-2613
New York, New York 10023

Ann Mitchell   (305)
1240 Biscayne Boulevard   422-1879
Miami, Florida 33162

HOW MUCH DO YOU KNOW?

1. Complete the Conversation

Tony: ....?
Tomiko: Yes, I read a lot.
Tony: ....?
Tomiko: All kinds, but especially mysteries.
Tony: ....?
Tomiko: Agatha Christie. What do you do in
            your free time?
Tony: .... and I go to the movies.
Tomiko: ....?
Tony: About once a month. ....?
Tomiko: Sure. I'd love to.

2. Find the Conversations

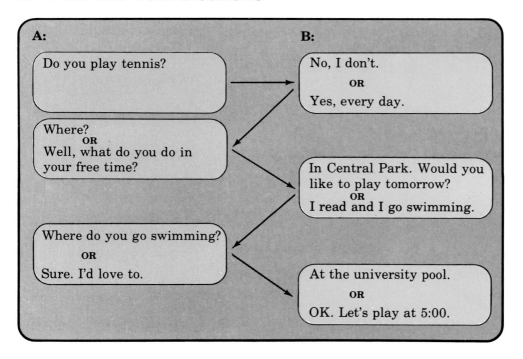

3. Find the answer and write the letter in the blank. Use each letter only once.

1. What's your name? ....
2. Where are you from? ....
3. Where do you live? ....
4. Who do you live with? ....
5. Do you just study, or do you work too? ....
6. What do you do in your free time? ....
7. What kind of movies do you like? ....
8. Who's your favorite actor? ....
9. How often do you go to the movies? ....
10. Would you like to go to the movies tonight? ....

a) Once a week.
b) I go to the movies.
c) I work too.
d) On 82nd Street.
e) Juan Sanchez.
f) I live with my family.
g) Mexico.
h) I'm sorry, I can't.
i) Westerns.
j) Clint Eastwood.

LANGUAGE SUMMARY

Now You Can Do This:

talk about likes and dislikes:	Do you like American TV? What kind of movies do you like? Who's your favorite actor?
ask how often:	How often do you go to the movies?
invite someone to do something:	Would you like to play tennis sometime?
accept an invitation:	Yes, I'd love to.
refuse an invitation:	I'm sorry, I can't.

Grammar

Like

Do you like	to read? football?

Go + ing Word

How often do you **go**	swimm**ing?**

Frequency Words

I	play tennis	**(about) once a** **every**	day. week. month.

Present Tense

I You We They	**like**	movies.
He She	**likes**	

Useful Words and Expressions

play (**v**)
love (**v**)
go (swimming)
•
movies
western
comedy
science fiction
war movie
musical
love story
biography
autobiography

mystery
actor
actress
tennis
soccer player
singer
author
composer
music
rock
jazz
disco
classical

pool
park
all kinds
Monday
Tuesday
Wednesday
Thursday
Friday
Saturday
Sunday
•
American
favorite

•
especially
about once a month
never
better
sometime
every day
tomorrow
•
how often
•
I'd love to.
Well

Making plans

Tomiko and Jeannette are at the American Language Institute.

Jeannette: Let's get something to eat. I'm hungry.

Tomiko: That's a good idea. Where?

Jeannette: Well, Jane's Coffee Shop has good hamburgers and Amy's has a good special.

Tomiko: How much is the special?

Jeannette: About four or five dollars. I can't remember.

Tomiko: That's pretty expensive. Where's Jane's Coffee Shop? Is it near here?

Jeannette: Yes. It's on the corner of 8th Street and Broadway.

Tomiko: Let's go there. But I can't stay long. I have to go to the store before I go home.

Answer *That's right* **or** *That's wrong.*

1. Tomiko isn't hungry.
2. Jeannette and Tomiko go to Jane's Coffee Shop.
3. Tomiko thinks the special at Amy's Restaurant is expensive.
4. Jane's Coffee Shop is near the American Language Institute.

**Suggest getting something to eat/drink
like this:**

Jeannette: Let's get something to eat.
Tomiko: That's a good idea. Where?
Jeannette: At Jane's Coffee Shop.

A: Let's get something to ....
B: That's a good idea. Where? *or* I'm sorry, I can't.
A: At ....

2 **Ask and say where places are like this:**

Tomiko: Where's Jane's Coffee Shop?
Jeannette: On the corner of 8th Street and Broadway.

A: Where's ....?
B: (It's) on ....

3 **Ask and say how much something is:**

Tomiko: How much is the special?
Jeannette: Four or five dollars.

A: How much is ....?
B: .... dollars.

4 **Complete the conversation and practice it with a partner.**

Jim: Let's get a sandwich.

Sue: ....
1. Who?
2. When?
3. Where?

Jim: ....
1. At the university.
2. At the University Coffee Shop.
3. At the University Bookstore.

Sue: ....
1. Where's that?
2. Who's that?
3. What's that?

Jim: ....
1. It's expensive.
2. It's a coffee shop.
3. It's near here.

Sue: ....
1. OK. See you later.
2. OK. Let's go.
·3. OK. Goodbye.

5 **Complete the conversation with the words from the list.**

| | | do |
| | | does |

Jeannette: Oh, look! There .... a soccer game
tomorrow night.

Tomiko: .... you .... soccer?

Jeannette: Yeah. My husband and his brother ....

Tomiko: .... you .... to games very often?

Jeannette: No. We .... pretty busy. We ....
about once or twice a month. Would you ....
to go sometime?

Tomiko: Sure.

do
does
're
's
play
plays
go
goes
like
likes

6 **Read the note and circle the correct answers.**

Tomiko,
I have to work late tonight and Toshi has to go to a party for the director of his company. There's some chicken in the refrigerator and I think there's some ice cream for dessert.
Can you get some tomatoes and lettuce to eat with the chicken? There's a store on 72nd Street near Broadway. Go there, it's cheap. Here's $10.00. Oh yes, and please get some cheese too.
See you between 10:30 and 11:00. thanks. Lynn

1. Paragraph (1) says
   a) There's some pie for dessert.
   b) Tomiko can eat chicken for dinner.
   c) There's a cheap store on 72nd Street.
2. Paragraph (2) says
   a) Tomiko can buy chicken.
   b) Tomiko can buy lettuce and tomatoes.
   c) Tomiko's cousin Toshi and his wife Lynn are busy.

7 **Complete the note.**

Please go to the _____
on _____
_____ and get some/a
_____ . Here's $_____ .
Thanks. _____
_____

Tomiko and Jeannette are at Jane's Coffee Shop.

Waitress:	**Are you ready to order?**
Tomiko:	**Yes. I'd like a chicken sandwich and a Coke.**
Jeannette:	**The same for me. And what kind of pie do you have?**
Waitress:	**Apple, lemon and chocolate.**
Jeannette:	**Apple, please.**
Tomiko:	**That's a good idea. Could I have a piece of apple pie too?**
Waitress:	**Sure. Is that all?**
Tomiko:	**Yes. I think so.**

Answer *That's right* **or** *That's wrong.*

1. Tomiko is not ready to order.
2. Jane's has lemon and chocolate pie.
3. Both Tomiko and Jeannette want a sandwich and a Coke.

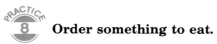

8 Order something to eat.

Waitress: Are you ready to order?
Tomiko: Yes. I'd like a chicken sandwich and a Coke.
Waitress: Is that all?
Tomiko: No. Could I have a piece of apple pie too?

A: Are you ready to order?
B: Yes. I'd like ....
A: Is that all?
B: No. Could I have .... too?

9 Ask what kind of food there is. Say what kind you want.

Jeannette: What kind of pie do you have?
Waitress: Apple, lemon and chocolate.
Jeannette: Apple, please.

A: What kind of .... do you have?
B: ....
A: ...., please.

10 Tomiko is ordering something to eat. Write *a* or *some*.

Tomiko: Could I have .... glass of water and
           .... salt, please?
Waitress: Sure.
Tomiko: And could I have .... piece of apple pie too?
Waitress: Would you like .... ice cream on your pie?
Tomiko: No, thanks. But I'd like .... milk for my coffee.

11 Complete the conversation and practice it with a partner.

Jeannette: What kind of ice cream do you have?

Waitress: ....
1. Yes, I do.
2. No, I have to go.
3. Chocolate and vanilla.

Jeannette: ....
1. Cheese, please.
2. Chocolate, please.
3. A large Coke, please.

Waitress: ....
1. Why?
2. That's OK.
3. Is that all?

Jeannette: ....
1. No, I don't like coffee.
2. No, I'd like some coffee.
3. No, I like coffee.

Waitress: ....
1. OK.
2. Not yet.
3. Why not?

Review on FOOD

OCTOBER 25, 1989

NEW YORK

GOOD FOOD

AROUND GREENWICH VILLAGE

By ANN ROCHETTE

There are many good restaurants and coffee shops in Greenwich Village where you can get everything from a snack to a complete meal.

JANE'S Coffee Shop

BREAKFAST	6:00 A.M. – 11:30 A.M.
LUNCH	11:30 A.M. – 2:00 P.M.
DINNER	5:00 P.M. – 7:30 P.M.

Sandwiches • Beverages • Desserts

TODAY'S SPECIAL
$5.95
Roast Beef
Served with salad, vegetables, dessert and coffee.

PRACTICE 12 Can you find the answers to these questions in the newspaper advertisement? Circle *yes* or *no*.

1. Where's Jane's Coffee Shop?   YES   NO
2. What time is breakfast?   YES   NO
3. How much is breakfast?   YES   NO
4. What kind of vegetables do you get with the special?   YES   NO
5. Do they serve desserts at Jane's?   YES   NO

PRACTICE 13 Take and give orders. You can say:

Are you ready to order?
What would you like?
Is that all?
Can I help you?

Some/A .... , please.
Some more .... , please.
Could I have .... ?
I'd like some/a ....

PRACTICE 14 **Find** *Coke, sandwich, salt, pie, hamburger, dessert, hot dog, coffee, sugar, milk, tea, cake, lettuce.*

```
O V H A M B U R G E R E R T E R S
C K L Y C O K E O S T I X O W
L B A S A N D W I C H O R M Y
X M I L K O E T R X O P R I M
N A P I E M S A L T T E A N I
Z I T R O S S I T O D O F I N
A C O M I N E X O C O F F E E
C E S U G A R Y N I G R O P E
T R O L L E T T U C E O S A R
```

Tomiko invites Jeannette to a movie.

Tomiko: **What do you do, Jeannette?**

Jeannette: **I'm a nurse. I work at General Hospital.**

Tomiko: **You work and study, and you're a housewife too? Where do you find the time?**

Jeannette: **Oh, I don't know. I even have some free time.**

Tomiko: **What do you do in your free time?**

Jeannette: **I read and I go to the movies.**

Tomiko: **Oh, I like movies too. Would you like to go tomorrow?**

Jeannette: **I can't tomorrow. I have to work. But I'd like to go sometime. How often do you go?**

Tomiko: **About twice a month.**

Answer *That's right* **or** *That's wrong.*
1. Jeannette is married.
2. Jeannette doesn't have any free time.
3. Tomiko would like to go to the movies with Jeannette.

15 **Ask someone what he/she does in his/her free time. Tell someone what you do in your free time.**

Tomiko: What do you do in your free time?
Jeannette: I read and I go to the movies? What
              about you?
Tomiko: I go swimming and I play tennis.

A: What do you do in your free time?
B: .... What about you?
A: ....

 16 **Invite someone to go somewhere. Accept or refuse an invitation.**

Tomiko: Would you like to go to the movies?
Jeannette: I can't. I have to work.

A: Would you like to go ....?
B: I can't. I have to .... *or* Sure. I'd love to.

 17 **Complete the conversation and practice it with a partner.**

Jeannette: What do you do in your free time?

Tomiko: ....
1. I go to work.
2. I play tennis.
3. I go to the office.

Jeannette: ....
1. Why not?
2. Where?
3. Who?

Tomiko: ....
1. At 8:00.
2. At a coffee shop.
3. In the park.

Jeannette: ....
1. I like to play tennis too.
2. I like to read too.
3. I like movies too.

Tomiko: ....
1. Let's go.
2. Really? Let's play sometime.
3. Let's get a sandwich.

**Jeannette and Tomiko are leaving Jane's Coffee Shop.
A man asks for some information. Look at the map and
complete the conversation with** *on, on the corner of,
across from, between, next to.*

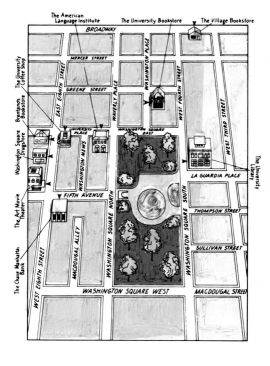

Man:	Is Brentano's near here?
Jeannette:	Yes, it's .... the University Coffee Shop.
Man:	And a bank?
Jeannette:	The Chase Manhattan Bank is .... Fifth Avenue and 8th Street.
Man:	And where can I find a drugstore?
Tomiko:	There's a drugstore .... 8th Street .... Fifth Avenue and University Place. It's .... the movie theater.
Man:	Thanks.
Tomiko:	You're welcome.

Read the letter to Tomiko's mother. Circle the correct answers.

October 11, 1989

Dear Mom,

(1) How are you and Dad? (2) Why don't you write? (3) I know you're
busy with your new job, but can't you send a post card sometime? (4) I miss
both of you.

(5) My English classes are great—especially now. (6) One of the guys in
my class is really nice. His name's Tony and he's from Brazil. (8) He works
in a restaurant and he wants to study business administration. (9) He likes
movies and sports—and guess what? (10) He plays tennis!

(11) I'd like to write more, but I have to go now. (12) It's 6:30 and my
class is at 7:00. (13) I'll write again tomorrow.

Love,

TOMIKO

1. *You* in sentence (1) refers to   a) Mom.   b) Dad.
2. *Both of you* in sentence (4) refers to   a) Mom and Dad.   b) Mom.
3. *One* in sentence (6) refers to   a) Tony.   b) the English class.
4. *My class* in sentence (12) probably refers to   a) Tomiko's English class.
   b) Tomiko's tennis class.

Plan a meal

I. Find out what "appetizer" means. _____
   What does "bran" mean? _____
   Find out what "muffins" means. _____
   What does "entree" mean? _____

II. Now plan your breakfast, lunch and dinner. Discuss your choices with a classmate.

Example:

Breakfast

Carrot juice   2 fried eggs with bacon
Papaya   Bran muffins

                        A glass of milk

Breakfast

_____juice   _____
                                                  (eggs or cereal)

_____   _____
        (fruit)   (bread)

                _____
                        (beverage)

Lunch

Appetizer: _____   Entree: _____
                                         Served with: _____

                                         _____
Soup: _____   Dessert: _____
Salad: _____   Beverage: _____

Dinner

Appetizer: _____   Entree: _____
                                         Served with: _____

                                         _____
Soup: _____   Dessert: _____
Salad: _____   Beverage: _____

Grammar Index

a/an 18

adverbs (frequency: sometime, once) 89

alphabet 26

articles
  definite (the) 60
  indefinite (a, an) 18

auxiliaries
  do 32, 39, 81
  does 32
  has to/have to 67

be
  am, is 6, 32
  are 6, 18, 32

can 60

count nouns 60, 73

definite article 60

do 32, 39, 81

does 32

frequency words 89

has to/have to 67

how
  how do you spell 32
  how often 89

indefinite article a/an 18

interrogative words (see question words)

mass nouns 60, 73

modals (modal auxiliaries)
  can 60
  would 73

numbers
  cardinal (1, 2, 3 . . .) 6, 8
  ordinal (1st, 2nd, 3rd . . .) 48

plurals
  regular/irregular 32

possessive adjectives 18, 32

prepositions: location 53, 60, 81

pronouns
  demonstrative 24
  indefinite 39
  personal 18, 24, 39

question words
  how 32, 89
  what 6, 12, 32, 67
  where 6, 60, 67
  who 81

short answers
  am 18, 32
  are 18, 32
  do 39
  is 24, 32

simple present tense 89

some 60, 73

the 60

there is/there are 53

what
  what course 6
  what do/does 32
  what's 12
  what time 67

where
  where can 67
  where is/are 6, 60, 67

who
  who do 81

wh questions (see how, what, where, who)

word order: statements/questions 24

would 73

yes/no questions
  are 18, 32
  do 39, 81, 89
  is 24, 32

Word List

The number beside each word tells you where the word first appears in the book.

A
a 8
about 1
accountant 14
across 54
actor 82
actress 84
actually 82
address 7
administration 14
advanced 50
advertisement 57
advertising 37
after 9
afternoon 2
again 54
age 34
agent 42
ago 26
air 15
airline 42
all 1
almost 49
alone 74
already 61
also 2
always 70
A.M. 58
am 14
American 3
an 14
and 1
answer 1
any 25
anybody 68
anyone 77
any time 54
apartment 7
apple 68
application 50
appointment 58
arch 21
architect 42
are 1
around 70
art 57
article 36
ask 2
at 9
attendant 42
auditorium 56
August 9
aunt 78

author 84
autobiography 83
avenue 7

B
back 33
back-to-school 57
bank 47
baseball 83
be 9
because 28
beef 64
before 58
beginning 50
better 82
between 51
beverage 64
bilingual 25
birth 3
blade 57
book 8
bookstore 47
boring 86
both 15
boyfriend 15
boutique 86
bread 70
breakfast 86
briefcase 20
brother 25
building 22
business 50
businessman 37
businesswoman 36
busy 35
but 9
butter 70
by 47
bye 7

C
cake 64
calculator 57
camera 57
campus 49
can 2
card 3
care 77
cents 61
certainly 77
chance 47

cheap 61
check 68
cheese 64
cheeseburger 64
chemist 37
chicken 64
child 32
children 32
chocolate 68
Christmas 77
city 7
class 9
classical 84
clean 70
coat 20
coffee 13
Coke 64
college 57
come 47
comedy 83
common 25
company 36
complete 70
composer 84
concert 85
conversation 3
corner 47
cosmetics 36
could 58
course 1
cousin 74
cup 42
cute 33

D
dance 83
dancing 85
date 3
daughter 15
day 7
dear 9
deodorant 55
department 57
dessert 64
devil 35
dictionary 20
die 26
different 28
dinner 65
direct 36
director 36
dish 70

dislike 83
disco 84
discount 57
divorced 26
do (**aux.**) 13
do (**v**) 13
doctor 17
does 25
dollars 90
don't 8
down 33
Dr. 44
dress 57
drink 62
drinking 56
driver 17
drugstore 49

E
eat 62
eight 6
eighteen 8
eighteenth 48
eighth 48
eighty 8
eighty-seven 8
either 61
elevator 54
eleven 8
eleventh 48
else 68
employee 37
enclosed 10
engineer 14
English 1
especially 82
even 96
evening 1
ever 74
every 70
everything 22
examination 10
example 70
excellent 57
except 42
exciting 86
excuse 1
executive 37
exercise 61
expensive 61
experience 77
extra 64

F

fabulous 86
fact 86
family 21
fantastic 46
fast 70
father 25
favorite 82
February 3
fiction 83
fifteen 8
fifteenth 48
fifth 9
fifty 8
fifty-four 8
film 55
finally 86
find 78
fine 21
finish 77
first 7
fish 64
fishing 85
five 3
flight 42
floor 54
food 61
football 85
for 9
foreign 14
form 7
forty 8
forty-three 8
fountain 56
four 3
fourteen 8
fourteenth 48
fourth 28
free 35
french fries 64
Friday 85
fried 64
friend 13
from 1

G

game 85
get 54
girl 35
girlfriend 45
glad 2
glass 68
go 19
good 2
goodbye 7
grade 15
graduate 28
great 98
guess 19

guest 71
guy 86

H

hamburger 61
happy 35
have 8
have to 61
he 2
hello 1
help 9
help (v) 54
her 8
here 7
hi 1
high school 28
him 28
his 8
historic 50
history 36
home 7
homework 61
hospital 96
hot dog 64
hotel 14
hour 50
house 74
housewife 27
how 4
hundred 8
hungry 61
husband 15

I

I 8
ice cream 64
idea 61
identification 3
if 45
I'll 33
I'm 1
impressive 22
in 1
include 70
independent 77
inexpensive 70
informal 70
information 9
institute 3
interesting 21
intermediate 50
international 9
invite 85
is 1
it 7
item 70
its 36

J

jazz 84
job 28
just 68

K

kind 68
know 13

L

ladies 33
language 3
large 37
last 7
later 7
lawyer 25
learn 77
least 50
leave 77
left 14
lemon 68
let's 19
letter 9
lettuce 64
library 56
life 77
like 54
like (v) 13
list 54
little 28
live 36
located 70
lonely 74
long 61
look 19
lot 21
love 21
love (v) 21
lovely 35
lucky 77
lunch 70

M

maiden 25
making 40
man 32
many 70
map 48
March 3
married 25
marry 78
May 3
maybe 58
me 1
meal 70
mean 25

meat 70
medical 15
medium 68
meet 1
men 32
menu 64
merchandise 57
milk 64
minute 33
Miss 9
miss (v) 21
mixed 64
Monday 57
month 7
moon 25
more 35
morning 2
most 28
mother 25
movie 49
Mr. 9
Mrs. 9
Ms. 9
much 54
museum 86
music 84
musical 83
my 1
myself 77
mystery 83

N

name 1
near 47
need 49
never 77
new 15
news 15
newspaper 15
next 5
next (to) 33
nice 1
night 74
nine 3
nineteen 8
nineteenth 48
ninety 8
ninety-eight 8
ninth 48
no 14
north 9
not 17
note 35
notebook 20
November 3
now 4
number 7
nurse 14

O

occupation 28
o'clock 10
October 3
of 7
off 57
office 36
often 35
oh 1
OK 1
old 33
on 9
once 82
one 6
one hundred 8
only 35
open 57
or 1
order 65
order (v) 68
other 70
others 77
our 32
out 65
outside 50
over 33

P

pants 57
parent 38
park 50
part 5
party 92
pen 20
pencil 20
people 2
perfect 70
phone 7
picture 21
pie 64
piece 68
pilot 42
place 3
placement 10
plans 90
play 82
player 84
please 5
P.M. 57
pocket 57
pool 88
post card 21
post office 49
potato 68
prefer 77
price 57
probably 98

profession 30
professional 50
program 9
pronunciation 50
purse 20

Q

question 4
quick 35

R

razor 57
read 3
ready 68
really (**adv.**) 19
really (**interjection**) 13
reasonable 70
receptionist 37
refrigerator 58
register 9
registration 7
remember 54
reservations 42
residence 9
resident 50
restaurant 13
retired 25
review 40
right 1
roast 64
rock 84
room 9
roommate 77

S

salad 64
sale 57
salesmen 27
salespeople 37
salt 69
same 42
sandwich 64
Saturday 85
save 57
say (**interjection**) 13
say (v) 2
school 15
science 83
second 28
secretary 13
section 95
see 7
send 35
separated 26
September 9
serve 95

served 64
server 71
seven 6
seventeen 8
seventeenth 48
seventh 48
seventy 8
seventy-six 8
seven-year-old 25
sex 7
shampoo 57
she 2
shirt 57
shoes 57
shop 42
sick 46
side 64
sign 7
signature 7
sincerely 9
sing 83
singer 84
single 26
sir 68
sister 25
sit 33
six 6
sixteen 8
sixteenth 48
sixth 48
sixty 8
sixty-five 8
skirt 57
slacks 57
small 64
snack 70
so 35
soccer 84
some 25
someday 77
someone 2
sometime 76
sometimes 74
something 61
somewhere 25
son 15
soon 36
sorry 19
special 50
spell 25
sports 83
square 9
staff 3
stay 61
store 57
strawberry 70
street 7
student 3
study 50

subway 74
successful 36
sugar 69
Sunday 74
supermarket 49
supplies 57
sure 33
sweater 20
swimming 85

T

take 70
talk 4
tax 71
taxi 17
tea 64
teach 28
teacher 4
telephone 7
television 29
ten 6
tennis 82
tenth 48
terrific 47
than 50
thank you 7
thanks 21
that 10
that's 1
the 3
theater 49
their 15
them 15
themselves 77
then 77
there 9
there's 19
these 25
they 21
think 13
third 15
thirteen 8
thirteenth 48
thirty 8
thirty-two 8
this 1
those 33
three 6
Thursday 57
time 3
tired 46
to 1
today 64
together 74
tomato 64
tomorrow 61
tonight 54
too 1

toothpaste 55
tourist 50
true 61
truly 87
Tuesday 85
tuna 64
TV 29
twelfth 48
twelve 8
twentieth 48
twenty 8
twenty-first 48
twenty-one 8
twice 85
twin 25
two 3
type 86

U
uh-huh 21
umbrella 20

uncle 13
university 3
until 57
unusual 42
up 86
uptown 82
used 57
usually 70

V
vanilla 70
vegetable 64
very 29
visa 50

W
waitress 14
wallet 20
want 69
watch 65

watch (**v**) 74
water 69
we 1
Wednesday 85
week 50
welcome 7
well (**interjection**) 27
well-known 36
we're 1
west 44
western 82
what 1
when 65
where 1
while 61
who 13
why 35
widow 77
widower 77
wife 15
with 15
woman 32

women 32
work 36
work (**v**) 13
worry 74
would 13
write 9
wrong 1

Y
yeah 13
year 7
yes 7
yet 69
you 1
young 77
your 3
yours 87
yourself 2

Z
zero 10
zip (code) 7